Sustainable Agriculture Applications Using Large Language Models

Edited by

Raghavendra M. Devadas

Manipal Institute of Technology Bengaluru
Manipal Academy of Higher Education
Manipal, India

Vani Hiremani

Symbiosis Institute of Technology
Symbiosis International (Deemed University)
Pune, India

&

Praveen Gujjar Jagannath, Lubna Ambreen & Harold Andrew Patrick

Faculty of Management Studies
JAIN (Deemed-to-be University)
Bengaluru, India

Sustainable Agriculture Applications Using Large Language Models

Editors: Raghavendra M. Devadas, Vani Hiremani, Praveen Gujjar Jagannath,
Lubna Ambreen & Harold Andrew Patrick

ISBN (Online): 979-8-89881-018-4

ISBN (Print): 979-8-89881-019-1

ISBN (Paperback): 979-8-89881-020-7

Published by Bentham Science Publishers Pte. Ltd., Singapore, in collaboration

with Eureka Conferences, USA

First published in 2025.

BENTHAM SCIENCE PUBLISHERS LTD.
End User License Agreement (for non-institutional, personal use)

need for a court order if at any point you breach any terms of this License Agreement. In no event will any delay or failure by Bentham Science Publishers in enforcing your compliance with this License Agreement constitute a waiver of any of its rights.

3. You acknowledge that you have read this License Agreement, and agree to be bound by its terms and conditions. To the extent that any other terms and conditions presented on any website of Bentham Science Publishers conflict with, or are inconsistent with, the terms and conditions set out in this License Agreement, you acknowledge that the terms and conditions set out in this License Agreement shall prevail.

Bentham Science Publishers Pte. Ltd.
No. 9 Raffles Place
Office No. 26-01
Singapore 048619
Singapore
Email: subscriptions@benthamscience.net

BENTHAM SCIENCE

CONTENTS

FOREWORD

In an era marked by rapid technological advancement and evolving agricultural challenges, the integration of technology into farming practices has become increasingly imperative. As we stand at the intersection of agriculture and innovation, the book "Sustainable Agriculture Applications Using Large Language Models" emerges as a beacon of insight and guidance for agricultural professionals, researchers, policymakers, and practitioners alike.

This book, meticulously crafted by a team of experts, offers a comprehensive exploration of how technological innovations, including Large Language Models (LLMs), can revolutionize sustainable farming practices. By delving into topics ranging from precision agriculture to data analytics and the ethical considerations surrounding technology adoption, the authors provide readers with a roadmap to navigate the complexities of modern agriculture.

At its core, this book embodies the spirit of collaboration and inclusivity, drawing upon diverse perspectives and real-world examples to illuminate the path forward. By showcasing the transformative potential of technology in agriculture, it inspires readers to embrace innovation while upholding principles of environmental stewardship and social responsibility.

As we embark on this journey of exploration and discovery, let us heed the insights offered within these pages and work together to cultivate a future where technology catalyzes sustainable agricultural development. May this book inspire meaningful change, empowering us all to build a more resilient, equitable, and prosperous agricultural landscape for generations to come.

Guru Prasad M.S.
Department of Computer Science and Engineering
Graphic Era (Deemed to be University)
Dehradun, India

PREFACE

Welcome to "Sustainable Agriculture Applications Using Large Language Models." This book represents a collaborative effort aimed at shedding light on the transformative potential of technology in agriculture and providing practical guidance for its integration into sustainable farming practices.

In recent years, the agricultural sector has faced unprecedented challenges, from population growth and resource depletion to climate change and food insecurity. In response, there has been a growing recognition of the need to embrace technological innovation as a means of addressing these challenges while promoting environmental sustainability and socio-economic development.

At the heart of this book lies a commitment to exploring the intersection of technology and agriculture, with a particular focus on the applications of Large Language Models (LLMs). Through a series of insightful chapters, we delve into topics such as precision agriculture, data analytics, and the ethical considerations surrounding technology adoption, offering readers a comprehensive understanding of the opportunities and challenges inherent in leveraging technology for sustainable farming.

Throughout this journey, we draw upon diverse perspectives and real-world examples to illustrate the potential impact of technology on agriculture and inspire readers to embrace innovation in their own farming practices. Whether you are a seasoned agricultural professional, a researcher exploring the frontiers of technology, or a policymaker shaping the future of agriculture, we hope that this book serves as a valuable resource and catalyst for positive change in the agricultural sector.

As we embark on this exploration together, let us remain mindful of the interconnectedness of our actions and the profound impact they have on the planet and its inhabitants. By harnessing the power of technology for sustainable farming, we could cultivate a future where agriculture thrives in harmony with nature, nourishing both people and the planet.

Raghavendra M. Devadas
Manipal Institute of Technology Bengaluru
Manipal Academy of Higher Education
Manipal, India

Vani Hiremani
Symbiosis Institute of Technology
Symbiosis International (Deemed University)
Pune, India

&

Praveen Gujjar Jagannath, Lubna Ambreen & Harold Andrew Patrick
Faculty of Management Studies
JAIN (Deemed-to-be University)
Bengaluru, India

List of Contributors

Beldona Visweswara	Department of CSE, Presidency University, Bangalore, India
Dudekula Sanjay	Department of CSE, Presidency University, Bangalore, India
Hemanth Kumar Shankarappa	Acharya Institute of Management and Sciences, Bengaluru, India
Indupuri Mohan Vamsi	Department of Computer Science and Engineering, Presidency University, Bangalore, India
Jayanthi Ethiraj	Department of CSE, Presidency University, Bangalore, India
Muchamari Vishnu Vardhan	Department of CSE, Presidency University, Bangalore, India
Napoleon Prabakaran	CMS Business School, JAIN (Deemed-to-be University), Bengaluru, Karnataka, India
Navaneethakumar Venugopal	CMS Business School, JAIN (Deemed-to-be University), Bengaluru, Karnataka, India
Shalini Acharya	School of Management, Presidency University, Bengaluru-560064, Karnataka, India
Sreelatha	Department of Computer Science and Engineering, Presidency University, Bangalore, India
Tintu Vijayan	Department of CSE, Presidency University, Bangalore, India
Tharun Darur	Department of CSE, Presidency University, Bangalore, India
Uma Chandrakant Swadimath	Faculty of Management Studies, CMS Business School, JAIN (Deemed-to-be University), Bengaluru, India
Vijaya Gangoor	CMS Business School, JAIN (Deemed-to-be University), Bengaluru, Karnataka, India
Veluswamy Saravana Kumar	Acharya Institute of Management and Sciences, Bengaluru, India

CHAPTER 1

Leveraging Artificial Intelligence in India's Food Processing Industries: Advancing Sustainable Agriculture through Large Language Models

Uma Chandrakant Swadimath[1,*] and **Shalini Acharya**[2]

[1] *Faculty of Management Studies, CMS Business School, JAIN (Deemed-to-be University), Bengaluru, India*

[2] *School of Management, Presidency University, Bengaluru-560064, Karnataka, India*

Abstract: Industrialisation and technological advancements are the key factors in a country's economic development. With the Industry 4.0 revolution, technology has given rise to inventions like Artificial Intelligence (AI), the Internet of Things (IOT), Blockchain technology, and Machine Learning (ML). These technological tools have been adopted in the key economic sectors, namely agriculture, industry, and service. Agriculture is a predominant sector in India's economic development. The share of the primary cultivation sector in India's economy was 18% in 2022-23. Changes in demand, lifestyles, and food habits have led to the development of food processing industries. The food processing industry is considered a sunrise industry in India. Food processing refers to a set of methods that are used to convert agricultural products into value-added products by retaining their nutritional value for consumption. It is an act of producing raw vegetables and seafood products that are transformed into consumable products with the help of labour, technology, and research-based information.

Artificial intelligence (AI) or Robotic intelligence (RI) refers to the integration of intelligence into machines that can operate with vision system that can detect product defects, control quality, differentiate products, and perform rejection during the production process. AI can be defined as an injection of humanity's brain power into appliances/instruments that are programmed to imagine and act like human beings, which is an outcome of scientific research and technological knowledge. The application of AI in the Indian food processing industry has become indispensable due to the issues of chemicals found in processed spice products produced by companies like MDH and Everest. Production of food products is a crucial factor in confronting the expectations of consumers and also due to the popularity of ready-to-eat foods as consumers have adapted themselves to the fast-paced working lifestyles. AI or robots are used at every stage of food production. The food processing industry ranks fourth in terms of the adoption of AI technology to maintain hygiene and control the quality of

---

* **Corresponding author Uma Chandrakant Swadimath:** Faculty of Management Studies, CMS Business School, JAIN (Deemed-to-be University), Bengaluru, India; E-mail: dr.uma_swadimath@cms.ac.in

Raghavendra M. Devadas, Vani Hiremani, Praveen Gujjar Jagannath, Lubna Ambreen & Harold Andrew Patrick (Eds.)

raw ingredients. The use of AI has become vital in the meat and dairy industries. Machine handling can help in identifying any damaged or contaminated processed food products and remove them from the production line. AI can help in reducing post-harvest losses and perishable wastages and increase the shelf life of processed food products. The Government of India has been encouraging the development of food processing industries. To support this development, it has also established food parks. The food parks have good warehousing facilities, rainwater harvesting, and cold storage facilities. With the availability of these infrastructural facilities and AI in these food parks, there is scope for food processing industries. The chapter examines the application of artificial intelligence in the food processing industries of India.

Keywords: Artificial intelligence (AI), Agro processing, Food parks, Food processing industries (FPIs), Technology.

INTRODUCTION

Agro processing includes the process of conversion of agricultural products and fishery products into consumable and edible products. It is a subset of the agricultural sector. The Food and Agricultural Organisation (FAO) uses the concept of food processing as agro-processing. It covers products from agriculture, horticulture, plantation, and ocean products. The concepts of agro-processing and food processing are synonymous. Agro-processing activities aim at product research, application of technological tools for agri-business development, raising the income of farmers, and promoting sustainable agricultural development. All of these are covered under food processing, where hi-tech machines are used to process agricultural products from the farm level.

The Food Processing Industry (FPI) is an emerging industry in India. FPIs are equipped with necessary infrastructural facilities that help in the reduction of waste, crop diversification, post-harvesting technologies, employment, add to export earnings, and better income to the farmers. India's agricultural sector is predominant, and it ranks second in the production of rice, wheat, fruits, and vegetables. It also ranks third in the production of milk, ghee, pulses ginger. With increased agricultural productivity and the supply of raw agricultural products, the FPI is growing at an average annual growth rate of 10%, which was previously just three percent. Food processing transforms agricultural produce into value-added products for consumption by consumers. It is an act of producing raw vegetables and seafood products that are transformed into consumable products with the help of labour, technology, and research-based information. The Food and Agricultural Organisation (FAO) uses the concept of FP as agro-processing. It covers products from agriculture, horticulture, plantation, and ocean products.

The Food and Drug Administration defines Food Processing (FP) as any food that includes any raw agricultural product that is subject to processing, canning, cooking, freezing, dehydration, and milling [1]. According to the Food and Agricultural Organisation (FAO), the FP includes all the activities to convert raw crops for consumption [2]. The Ministry of Food Processing Industries (MOFPIs), Government of India, has classified FP into manufactured processes and value-added processes. The manufactured process is concerned with the activity of transforming products of agriculture, animal husbandry, and fisheries into an edible form with the utilization of labour, capital, power, and machinery, whereas value-added process is concerned with creating significant value-addition in terms of tastes, nutrition, and flavor that are ready for consumption purpose [3]. According to the Food Standards Agency, the food industry includes farming, food production, packaging, distribution, retailing and catering [4]. The FPI includes agricultural, horticultural, plantation, and marine products. There are three stages of food processing namely primary processing, secondary and tertiary processing. In the primary processing stage, raw agricultural products go through different stages of cleaning, grading, sorting, and packaging, which are ready for consumption. The FPIs have attracted foreign direct investment amounts of 6.36 billion US dollars till June 2023 which has increased to 12.58 billion US dollars in March 2024. The exports of processed food products increased from 4.9 billion US dollars to 13.01 billion dollars in 2022-23, indicating a growth of 13 percent [5]. The agricultural or food products are transformed into processed food products and supplied to the retail sector for final consumption under the secondary and tertiary. Previously, it was confined only to the preservation of foods, packaging, and transportation, but today, its scope is enlarged to the production of new ready-to-eat food, beverages, processed and frozen fruits/vegetables, and marine and meat products due to the advancement in innovative technology and Artificial Intelligence (AI). The 21st century has witnessed enormous changes in the technology field, with rapid developments in the Internet of Things (IoT), machine learning, blockchain technology, and AI. Food processing industries (FPIs) are gradually using AI technologies to improve the efficiency and quality of processed food products. AI technology has revolutionised businesses across all economic sectors, and its application has been increasing over recent years. Some issues faced by Everest and MDH products, the use of AI has become necessary to monitor the quality of raw materials, to improve operational efficiency and to deliver the products on time to the consumers. The use of AI in FPIs will help in the reduction of food wastage by 127 billion dollars by 2030. AI has engulfed businesses by transforming them and function efficiently. AI in the FPI aligns the production process with the demand and preferences/tastes of consumers. AI helps maintain the accuracy of food labelling and packaging of processed food products.

REVIEW OF LITERATURE

John R. Baldwin and David Sabourin (2002) analysed how technology is used in the Canadian food processing industry. They emphasize the use of technology in controlling the quality of products, particularly in the dairy, fruits, and vegetable processing industries [6]. NITI AAYOG (2018) has formulated a national strategic framework for the development of AI. Technological developments and transformation are happening due to constant research. AI has revolutionized the technology economy and to keep par with its developments, national strategies are initiated in all socio-economic sectors [7]. Scientific Information Bulletin (SIB) (2020), has illustrated the AI and deep learning applications in the food industry. It shows how deep learning technique is used in sorting, grading, and classifying food products into different grades [8]. Lili Zhu, Petros Spachos, Erica Pensini, and Konstantinos N. Plataniotis (2021) have highlighted how machine vision, such as image processing and remote sensing images, are used in food processing industries. They have stressed image processing, which can identify the types of food products and check the quality of food products [9]. In the machine vision system, a follow-up design is used for grading food products, detecting foreign particles, and removing impurities (MOFPI) (2021). The government of India elaborates and discusses the policy support and development initiatives for skill development infrastructure and setting up of micro food processing units and to provide technological infrastructure, cold chain storage facilities and AI tools for food parks established in the country. Sanya Talwar (2021) has outlined the importance of AI in FPIs and how machine learning can be used to protect crops, increase crop productivity, and provide better inputs for food processing, and an efficient use of AI will prevent wastage of food production [10]. Nidhi Rajesh Mavani, Jarinah Mohd Ali, Suhaili Othman, *et al.* (2021), analyze the benefits, significance, and limitations of AI in the food industry. AI applications are useful in the categorization of food products, predicting demand, and checking the quality of produced food products. AI can perform various tasks, such as determining the quality of food, categorizing food, and predicting demand in the market economy. They have examined how AI tools such as electronic noses, computer vision systems, machine learning, knowledge-based expert systems will benefit FPIs [11]. Rubina Romanello and Valerio Veglio (2022) have analysed the challenges and benefits of using industry 4.0 technologies in the food processing industries and agri sector in Italy. The use of Industry 4.0 technologies has resulted in better operations and management of human resources and has enabled the development of new strategies. AI helps in the reduction of food waste and emission of carbon-di-oxide [12]. Food Vision Report (2023) by the Food Future Foundation has shared a vision for food system transformation in India, which is aligned with the United Nations Food System. It discusses how food production has caused degradation of the environment, such as soil erosion, loss of biodiversity, climate change, and water and air pollution. It also relates to the agricultural sector and food processing industries in India [13]. Sudeep Srivastava (2024) has described how the integration of AI in the food industry has resulted in transforming traditional agricultural practices and food production processes, enhancing food safety standards, better supply chain management, and reduction in operational costs [14].

Research Gap

The growth of FPI has increased to 11.18 percent. Food processing involves various stages of processing, such as primary, secondary and tertiary processing. If processed food products are increased, there is also a wastage of these products. The quality of food is one of the concerns. Changes in lifestyles have led to the rise of demand for convenient food products such as ready-to-cook, ready-to-eat products. Growing technology has enabled FPIs to adopt modern technology methods to produce high-quality processed food products. Since AI is an emerging trend in all economic sectors, the study examines the scope of AI in FPIs such as quality control and food safety. Though technology is used in many FPIs to create value addition and increase the shelf life of the products and storage facilities, with the advent of AI, there can be better post-harvest practices and food safety control measures and help in the reduction of wastage. As a matter of fact, investment in AI is a costly affair and most of the food processing activities are operated manually, but with the help of AI, food quality can be checked, it can identify defects and reduce contamination of processed food products. There are gaps in supply chain management, storage, and distribution facilities. The present study is undertaken to identify the areas of AI in food processing and analyses its extent of implementation.

Theoretical Background

Knowledge-based expert system theory can be related to the use of AI in FPIs [15]. A knowledge based system is a computer program that acquires knowledge data and information from various sources to apply in a particular process or stage in food processing (Szturo K, Szczypinski PM,2017). The knowledge-based theory consists of areas, namely knowledge-based expert systems, artificial intelligence and research-based industrial science [16]. It refers to the decision-making ability of humans that can be imitated by devices and is referred to as Artificial Intelligence (AI). An internet-based tool is used to calculate the nutritional value of the food produced (Sipos A,2020). The application of a knowledge-based expert system is a prototype information technology where factors such as food safety, nutrition, and quality are studied [17]. Another digital learning technique, MESTRAL, was introduced in FPIs to assist in food science and technology [18]. Machine learning is a computer program categorized into supervised, unsupervised, and reinforcement learning [19]. Supervised learning refers to the prediction of the desired output from a given level of inputs, and unsupervised learning only classifies the given data. Reinforcement learning is an interaction between a program and the environment [20]. Long short-term memory, an AI tool is used in the food industry to detect water quality in the cheese fermentation process [21]. An electronic nose is a device to detect odors or flavours similar to the human nose [22]. This device consists of electronic chemical sensors that can recognize odors, which is helpful in checking the quality of food produced [23]. An electronic nose is a software component of pattern recognition algorithms where the response is processed. An electronic nose is used for classification, detection, and quality control of wines, grains, edible oils, eggs, dairy products, vegetables, meat and seafood products, and beverages [24]. It also helps in detecting contamination in processed food products [25].

Another theory can be related to the 'Decoupling Point' stated by Hoekstra S and Romme J. Due to changes in food habits and the demand of people, FPIs aim at producing processed food products as preferred by a large number of people. Decoupling Point indicates how consumer preferences in terms of choice for a large variety of processed food products lead to market penetration. This includes all activities of FPIs, such as procurement, production, sorting, storage, quality check, and distribution of processed food products to the consumers. The decoupling point relates to order-driven, inventory /procurement, and forecast-driven activities. All of these activities have to go through safety, technical and regulatory compliances [26]. The model of innovation and economic theory of technological change discusses the integration of invention in economic analysis. It relates to patents and the indivisibility of invention, which means that once a new procedure begins, it can be circulated to all the units to realize profits. Invention is one of the capital goods, and it is a new method of production and a public good. In the model of the invention, it says that the inventor has the exclusive right and license to use the invention for T years, and later, the invention becomes a public commodity [27]. There is another application of economic theory in information technology research. The theory has identified six areas where economic theory can be applied to information technology research, which include information economics, economics of information technology supply, information technology and organizational performance, industrial organization, institutional economics, and the macroeconomic impact of information technology. Developments in information technology have led to a transformation of how organizations work and how to maximize the return on technology investment [28].

TECHNOLOGY REVOLUTION

The term Artificial Intelligence (AI) was first coined by John McCarthy. According to him, AI is the science and engineering of making intelligent machines, which includes software programs. It possesses the skills of a human brain and executes the tasks intelligently. The objective of AI is to make machines learn and observe from humanity [29]. The concept of AI was introduced in 1940 in various forms of computing models. The intelligence-based computing method was introduced by Alan Turing in 1947. AI is a machine that can perform day-to-day applications and solve problems with intelligence that is embedded and programmed with a list of instructions by human intelligence. This is one of the essential products of Industry 4.0, which also includes machine learning and blockchain technology. The word 'Machine Learning' was introduced by Artur Samuel in 1959, which meant the ability to learn. It uses algorithm data, and with a given set of instructions for a particular task, the machine gets trained and performs specific tasks [30]. Deep learning is another technique used to implement machine learning. Machine learning understands the patterns in data and makes predictions of future data or trends [31]. AI, which is a disruption in the new technology, can perform tasks like humans. It has evolved itself into a variety of tasks which increases productivity and adds precision. AI adoption has become imperative for emerging economies; it is more often driven from a commercial perspective. Currently, countries are aware of the merits of AI; for instance, China and the United Kingdom have estimated that nearly 26% and 10% of their Gross Domestic Product (GDP) will be generated from AI-related economic activities. This can be possible through funding for research, digital infrastructure connectivity, and the AI ecosystem.

AI in FPIs at the Global Levels

The global food processing industry is witnessing tremendous change due to rapid technological innovations, AI, Robotic intelligence, machine learning, and digital food platforms. The market size of the global food processing industry is estimated to increase from 11 billion dollars in 2023 to 22.3 billion dollars by 2032, at a compound annual growth rate (CAGR) of 8.3%. (Chart **1**).

Table **1** shows the size of the food processing market globally using AI in FP activities. The global food processing market consists of fruits and vegetables, dairy, meat and poultry, convenience food, and snacks. The market size of FPI globally, which was 10.3 billion dollars, is estimated to increase to 22.3 billion dollars by 2032 with a compounded annual growth rate of eight percent.

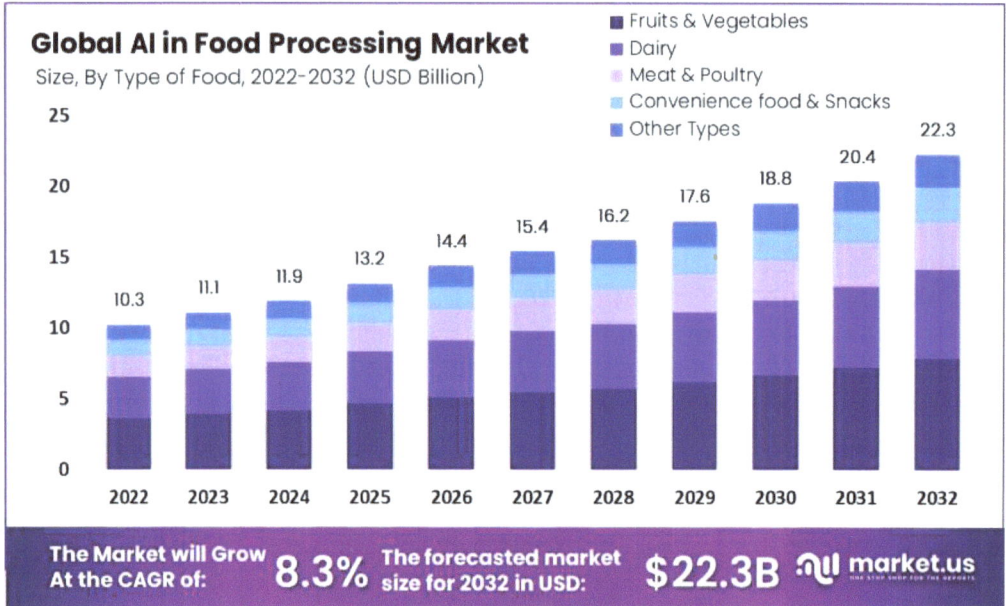

Global AI in Food Processing Market
Size, By Type of Food, 2022-2032 (USD Billion)

Legend:
- Fruits & Vegetables
- Dairy
- Meat & Poultry
- Convenience food & Snacks
- Other Types

Values by year: 2022: 10.3, 2023: 11.1, 2024: 11.9, 2025: 13.2, 2026: 14.4, 2027: 15.4, 2028: 16.2, 2029: 17.6, 2030: 18.8, 2031: 20.4, 2032: 22.3

The Market will Grow At the CAGR of: **8.3%** The forecasted market size for 2032 in USD: **$22.3B** market.us

Chart 1. Source: Market research report on AI in food processing market (2024), https://market.us/report/ai-in-food-processing-market/

Table 1. Categories of food processing.

Category	The Total Value of World Imports, USD Billion	The Total Value of India'S Exports, USD Billion	India Market Share (%)	India Ranking	World Leader	World Leaders' Share of Market (%)
Processed fruits and vegetables	52.4	0.5	0.9	18	China	15.6
Processed fish and seafood	97.2	4.4	4.6	6	China	14.6
Meat	101.8	1.7	1.6	10	USA	12
Dairy products	77.9	0.2	0.3	35	New Zealand	14.3
Poultry and eggs	24.7	0	0.2	61	Brazil	22.2

Source: Food Future Foundation (2024), Food Vision Report 2030.

North America occupies a dominant position in AI globally, as it is a key player in technology infrastructure and research developments through innovation. It emphasizes food safety and quality control and regular conformity to food regulations and standards [32]. It is observed that AI not only helps in food production but can also analyze consumer preferences to a larger extent and produce tastier products for them. For instance, in the USA, Coca-Cola has installed self-service soft drink fountains, which allow people to personalise their choice of drink. These fountains are programmed with AI software that can relate to consumer tastes and preferences [33]. With the help of AI sensors, the cleaning process in FPIs of the United Kingdom has saved energy and water up to 50% and increased productivity. Starbucks, through its app, analyses past orders, preferences, and location information to make customized food and drinks for its consumers.

Nestle also uses AI to analyse its trends and customers' inputs to provide food products that satisfy them. A food tech startup in Switzerland has developed a surveillance system using drones to understand changes in crops, fertilizers, pests, and agricultural output using computer vision, which is one of the AI tools [34].

Strategic Framework for AI development in India

AI adoption and application is the need of the hour for both advanced and emerging economies. New technology strategic objectives and plans are being made, focusing on investment in AI and leveraging its developments. In this context, NITI AAYOG, Government of India, has formulated a strategic framework for AI development, which is categorized into three interrelated components, namely opportunity, AI for Greater Good, and AI Garage [35].

The three components can be discussed in the following:

Opportunity: Economic Impact of AI

Among the economic factors of production—namely land, labour, capital, and organization—technological advancements have led to increased emphasis on capital investment, improved technical efficiency of labour, and enhanced productivity. The adoption of AI, which is the new norm in the field of production, has emerged as a new economic and technological factor input. AI can increase growth and productivity through intelligent automation, perform complex tasks, replace manual labour, and thereby enhance efficiency in the economic sectors.

AI for Greater Good: Social Development and Inclusive Growth

Greater good implies an improvement in the quality of life. For instance, greater access to healthcare facilities, inclusive financial growth and increased agricultural productivity, creation of smart cities, and technology infrastructure development through AI adoption all meet the demand of people.

AI Garage for 40% of the World

This refers to the adoption of AI in the healthcare sector. 40% of the world means ascertain AI healthcare solutions for 40% or more of the world that can be used in countries of Africa. AI technologies are not only focused on healthcare but also on agriculture, FPI and education. India is a benchmark for information technology development which can provide solutions and quality education to some of the developing countries. India is often referred to as the food basket of the world, the agricultural sector, which remains a predominant sector, is expected to meet the global demand for food by 50% and help feed an additional two billion people by 2050. This can be possible through smart farming, protection of crops by early detection of pest attacks by using drones and AI, and also encouraging FPIs. There are sensors to detect the quality of processed food products.

AI in FPIs of India

AI is the newest in the present technology revolution. AI is a technical machine where human-like intelligence is embedded, which can learn, act, detect and perform difficult tasks. With changing demand, lifestyles and food habits, there is a lot of potential for AI in the FPIs as it helps in classification, quality control, sorting, food safety norms, detection of food-borne diseases, and monitoring every food processing activity. All of these can be done with the help of food sensors [36]. India's FPI accounts for 32% of the total food market, as it is the largest producer of agricultural products. India's economy being agrarian in nature there is a huge potential for the growth of FPIs. The Government of India has emphasized the development of computer technology, such as (IoT) and AI applications in the FPIs. The use of these technologies will help in the reduction of crop waste, better crop yields, and improve the incomes of farmers. The Government of India has set up an Inter-Ministerial committee to formulate strategies for technology infrastructure, reduction in perishable wastage and improve the global competitiveness of the FPIs.

As per the India Business and Trade report, India's FPI may increase to 8.8% during 2024-2032. Due to the AI revolution, there is an integration of agriculture and the production of processed food products to the consumption of these products. Technological advancements and AI adoption are facilitating the production of quality processed foods and better incomes for farmers. Food processing activities include canning, freezing, fermenting and packaging, *etc.* The FPI of India is expected to produce 535 billion US dollars by the end of 2026. It contributes to 10.4% of exports and employs 11% workforce. It has attracted foreign direct investment to the extent of 12.5 billion dollars from April 2000 to December 2023 [37].

The Government has encouraged an investment of Rs.68000 crores in FPIs. It is considered a priority sector under the Make in India program. One hundred percent of foreign investment is allowed in the food industry. The Government has introduced Pradhan Mantri Kisan Sampada Yojana to invest and adopt world class infrastructure in FPIs. FPIs have forward and backward linkages. When these industries meet the increasing demand and invite investment, this is known as forward linkage, whereas food processing is related to research and development, cold chain and storage infrastructure, logistics and supply chain, and food start-ups. All of these comprise backward linkages. Due to the production of processed food products, agri-related exports have increased to 23% from 13% in 2014, resulting in India occupying the seventh position in the exports of processed foods in 2022-23.

India is the largest producer of fruits; it is the second largest producer of rice. The share of India's market in categories of processed fruits and vegetables, processed fish and seafood, meat, dairy products, poultry, and eggs has been 0.9%m, 4.6%, 1.6%, 0.3%, and 0.2%, respectively. India ranks sixth in processed fish and seafood products, but it ranks 61 in poultry and egg production. China leads India in processed fruits, vegetables, fish and seafood products [38].

Utilisation of Technology in Food Parks for the Growth of Agribusiness

The MOFPI encourages the establishment of food parks across the country under the Mega Food Park scheme. These food parks provide advanced technology and infrastructural facilities for food processing activities. They provide cold storage infrastructure, sorting, grading and processing centres, product development centres and quality control lab centres, and AI technologies [39].

There are around 24 food parks that are operational in the country. These food parks have a cold storage capacity of 8.4 lakh metric tonnes. Cold storage facilities and post-harvest technologies are essential requirements for FPIs. The Government of India has encouraged the development of food parks under the Mega Food Park scheme. These food parks are developed with the latest state-o--the-art processing facilities that include technologies like cold chain infrastructure, logistics and supply chain management, regular water and power supply, *etc.* The food parks have three major centres, namely collection, primary processing and central processing centres. The MOFPI has introduced an Integrated Cold Chain (ICC) scheme to provide cold chain infrastructure to the existing food parks in the country.

Cold storages are categorised into different technical standards such as pre-cooling, multi-commodity cold storage and control atmosphere storage. Cold chain storage infrastructural development is an integral part of food technology.

Multi-commodity cold storage has multiple layers to store a large variety of fruits and vegetables at different temperature levels. This includes individual quick freezing, mobile pre-cooling vans, reefer trucks and irradiation facilities. Individual quick-freezing technology supports the storage of seasonal fruits and vegetables, where each fruit or vegetable is kept in separate storage. Pre-cooling is another technique that removes heat from agricultural produce before it is put into cold storage, which helps retain the freshness of the produce and long shelf life. Mobile pre-cooling vans are electrically operated; these vans can produce around 20,000 square meters of cold air per hour to cool the produce after post-harvesting. Another modern technology used in the cargo area is the reefer, or refrigerated truck, which protects products that are sensitive to temperatures above a certain level. Irradiation facility is a technique that preserves food, reduces the risk of food-borne diseases, and prevents the spread of pests. The mega food park scheme is aimed to create modernized processing and preservation units, which will increase the level of processing and value addition of processed food products and also help to reduce production wastage. Under this scheme, a capital grant of 35-50% was given, and as of February 2021, 145 projects were approved. Another scheme introduced by the MOFPI is the scheme of integrated cold chain and value addition infrastructure. The objective is to provide cold chain and preservation facilities to the existing food parks in the country, and this scheme includes other facilities such as pre-cooling, sorting, grading and multi-product and multi-temperature cold storage. Mobile cooling units are set up that distribute marine, poultry, meat, and dairy products. Currently, there are 371 cold chain projects, 68 agro-processing clusters, and 186 food testing laboratory projects that have been approved under the expansion of food processing and preservation capacities.

Table **2** indicates that there are 250 integrated pack houses, 800 ripening chambers, cold storage facilities with a capacity of 32 million tonnes and less than ten thousand reefer trucks that exist in the food parks of the country. Integrated pack houses are those where horticultural produce is stored, cleaned, separated, packed, and stored in a hygienic environment. This helps maintain the freshness of the products suitable for export.

Food quality is very important for ensuring food safety. The Ministry of Food Processing has introduced quality checks and regulatory compliances for processed food products with the use of advanced technology and production.

a. Hazard Analysis and Critical Control Points (HACCP) is a food safety measure introduced in 1960. Based on the modern scientific food system, it prevents hazards during all stages of food production. These hazards may relate to biological, chemical, and physical threats during the production and processing of food products. All processed food products are authenticated under HACCP to promote international trade and food safety.

b. Food Safety And Standards Act of 2006 (FSSAI):The Government of India passed this act for proper compliance with food laws. This act serves as a single reference point for all issues related to food safety and standards. It addresses all the activities, such as the production, processing, storage, distribution, and marketing of processed food products. It is applicable to all categories of processed food products that, include bakery products, snacks and sweets, instant ready-to-eat, ready-to-cook, beverages, cereal products, confectionery products, frozen and canned marine products, *etc* [40].

Table 2. Availability of facilities in the food parks.

S. No.	Component	Existing Capacity
1	Integrated Pack Houses	250 numbers
2	Reefer Trucks	< 10,000 numbers
3	Cold store (Bulk & distribution hubs)	32 million tonnes
4	Ripening Chambers	800 numbers

Source: Annual Report (2023), Ministry of Food Processing Industry (MOFPI), Government of India.

GOVERNMENT SCHEMES FOR THE DEVELOPMENT OF FOOD PROCESSING INDUSTRIES

- The Ministry has introduced 'PM formalization of Micro Food Processing Enterprises (PMFME) scheme as part of Aatmanirbhar Bharat Abhiyan, which aims to provide financial, technical and business support for setting up and the upgradation of micro food processing enterprises. The scheme will bring in micro-enterprises of the unorganized sector of food processing and thereby provide them with all the required support to increase competitiveness. This scheme allows for capital investment, setting up of incubation centres, training, research and development, marketing, and branding in order to reinforce backward and forward linkages of FPIs [41].

- To ensure adequate allocation of resources, the Government has introduced 'One District One Product' (ODOP), which facilitates procurement of raw inputs, availing common infrastructural services and marketing of processed food products. This scheme can be used for selected products, namely agri produce, cereal based product or traditional food products. Under this scheme, the

National Institute of Food Technology Entrepreneurship and Management (NIFTEM) has prepared 760 training modules and has provided 190 course handouts.

- In order to increase production, processing and value addition of processed food products, the Government has introduced the creation or expansion scheme for food processing and preservation. This scheme encourages post-harvest processing, modernization of existing FPIs and improve the quality of end products.
- The Government has introduced the 'Operation Greens' scheme to encourage farmer-producer organisations, agri-logistics and processing facilities. This scheme was introduced as a part of Aatmanirbharat Bharat with an outlay of Rs. 500 crores. This scheme was extended to specific vegetables, namely tomato, onion and potato and to all fruits. This scheme has long-term intervention, which relates to the development of integrated value chain development projects and short-term interventions related to the reduction of post-harvest losses.
- To emphasise the adoption of AI and technology, the Government has introduced a Production Linked Incentive scheme where an amount of Rs. 10,900 crores has been allotted to the food processing industries. There is also another scheme known as Pradhan Mantri Kisan Sampada Yojana (PMKSY) which provides financial support to the FPIs and food parks for the development of integrated cold chain infrastructure and technology upgradation. This scheme encourages the adoption of machine learning, which helps in analyzing crop cultivation and productivity.
- The Government has introduced the Food Processing Industry Technology Upgradation Fund Scheme (FPTUFS), which is intended to upgrade processing facilities mainly for fruits and vegetables, dairy products, meat and poultry, cereals and fishery products. This scheme is not applicable to packaged drinking water and soft drink plants. This scheme also allows for setting up new plants and machinery and common infrastructure in the FPIs.

SCOPE FOR AI IN FOOD PROCESSING INDUSTRIES (FPIs)

AI is reshaping the economic sectors, particularly the agricultural and food processing sectors. AI has become necessary to produce better yields, maintain nutrition and contribute towards environmental sustainability. AI has entered the FPI, food delivery responding to demand changes of consumers. AI technologies such as machine learning, computer vision, and data analytics are applied to enhance efficiency, productivity, and safety in food processing industries. It can detect defects, contaminants and spoilage in real time of processed food products and improve quality [42].

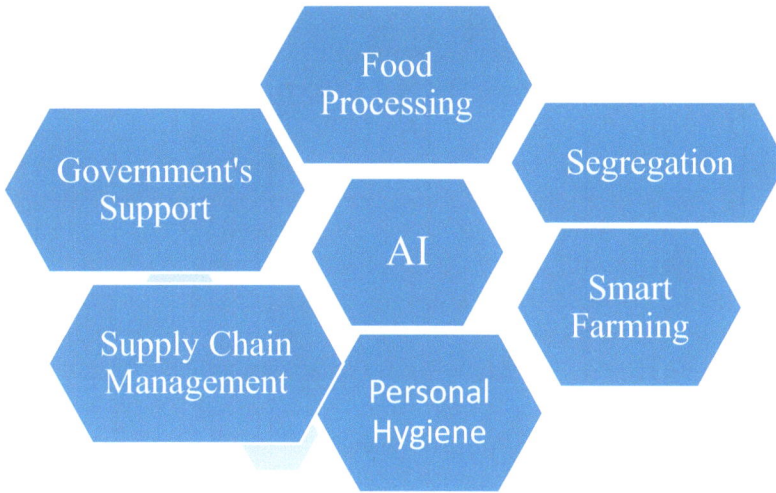

Chart 2. Source: Authors' description.

Segregation of Raw Agri and Horticultural Products

Food processing necessitates sorting and grading of a large quantity of feedstock and a thorough check of the end product, and this needs proper maintenance of the equipment and proper warehousing facilities (Chart **2**). Earlier, sorting was carried out using manual labour, but now this process is automated.

AI application in food processing industries helps in sorting raw agri / horticultural products as they come in various sizes and shapes and in huge quantities. Segregating or sorting these raw agri / horticultural products such as vegetables and fruits, if done manually, consumes many hours of labour but with the use of AI automation, sensor-based technology will reduce the number of hours, maintain quality, reduce labour cost, increase the speed of segregation of these raw products thereby reducing waste and improve production. AI-based tools are used to test the quality of inputs; it uses optical fluorescence and ultrasonic sensing imaging technologies to understand how much microbial debris and food is left in the machines during segregation and production [43]. AI machines can scan, inspect and identify any errors in the products and improve the quality of processed food products. Robots can help in sorting horticultural produce and put the same in separate containers. They also help in cutting fruits and vegetables which can be used in fast cooking. Robots can organize processed food products for storage and shipment.

Smart Farming

Smart farming is a new technological method used in agricultural fields, which again includes IoT and big data to monitor farming activities. This helps in detecting plant/ crop diseases, and environmental changes like temperature and soil fertility [44]. It helps farmers in predicting weather conditions which in turn helps them in planning crop cultivation. AI can identify weeds where chemicals are sprayed only on the weeds without affecting the cultivated crops. This kind of information is collected by farmers using sensors and drones, which helps in improving the quality of agricultural products that can be processed easily, maintain nutrition and reduce waste. NITI Aayog and IBM have collaborated to develop a crop yield prediction tool using AI, which improves farm productivity, provides insights into soil fertility, and issues early warning on pests causing crop diseases through remote sensing. This project is implemented in the states of Assam, Bihar, Jharkhand, Madhya Pradesh, Maharashtra, Rajasthan and Uttar Pradesh. Doubling Farmers' Income, which is the nation's objective, AI adoption focuses on efficient supply chain management and market development by increasing productivity.

Personal Hygiene

With the outbreak of the pandemic, the concept of personal hygiene was emphasized and the labourers and employees in FPIs had to compulsorily wear face masks, head caps and hand gloves to ensure food safety. Some software companies have developed AI and ML applications that have face recognition apps that monitor employees to see whether they are following hygiene compliances or not during the production process. The quality of processed food products is important in the food industry, and it is essential that food safety norms and compliances are followed. There are sensors to check the quality of processed food products. To ensure this quality inspection, AI machines can be used, where food products are scanned, inspected, and monitored so that quality is not diluted and the nutritional content of the food products [45]. An AI powered vision quality is used, where the entire quality process is monitored.

AI Helps Supply Chain Management in FPIs

AI helps in monitoring supply chain management from the agricultural fields, to warehousing and processing centres. It adds to better inventory management, maintenance of warehousing and processing centres and maintain safety. AI helps in the transportation of processed food products by using sensors, a global positioning system to track the movement and reduce the risk of food-related diseases. The use of automation and AI in FPI will increase the shelf life of processed food products. As there have been instances of lack of food safety automation becomes helpful to check the quality of ingredients and products. AI and robotics are used in food production and packaging of processed food products. AI is used in FPI for product testing, inventory management, tracking of products from harvest to distribution and monitoring the compliance of food safety regulations. Robots are used in packaging processed food products by assembling packaged products like frozen products, marine products, agri products. These robots will place food in containers for better storage, maintaining the shelf life and shipment. This, in turn, will be helpful in the distribution of the products with less time consumption. Biodegradable packaging and smart food packaging maintain the quality of products and help consumers with product information. The use of AI improves supply chain management through the following ways, which are testing processed food products at every level from the processing stage till its final stage, managing inventory, keeping track of the products from harvest to distribution and maintaining hygiene standards. It assists in the mitigation of foodborne illnesses. An important benefit of AI in FPIs, it helps to reduce food wastage. It can identify whether fruits are ripe and harvesting of agricultural produce.

Government's Support

The Government of India, the Ministry of Electronics and Information Technology, and the National Institute of Food Technology Entrepreneurship and Management have emphasized the using AI technologies in agriculture and FPIs. As the use of AI in FPI is in its infant state, the Government stressed the need to create a roadmap for its development. The Government encourages the setting up of processing clusters, promotes research and development and innovations in producing different processed foods, maintains food safety and sets up food testing laboratories. The FPI is considered a priority sector under the Make in India programme. The Government has introduced Pradhan Mantri Kisan Sampada Yojana and Pradhan Mantri Kisan Sampada Yojana t to invest in infrastructure and other technologies for FPIs with an investment of Rs. 68000 crores.

CHALLENGES OF AI IN THE FPIs

Though there are so many advantages of AI in the FPIs, there are also challenges in the FPIs.

Firstly, there is a lack of awareness of implementing AI, as this involves training in AI machines, systems and applications. The cost of AI implementation is high when the FPIs want to adopt AI technologies and make the process completely automated. This includes investing in data collection and storage systems, high-speed internet connectivity, and advanced machinery equipped with AI capabilities. Investment in AI technologies is expensive and there is a huge demand for AI-enabled skilled workers. There is a threat of loss of employment because if food processing is automated on a large scale, AI will replace manual work. Adoption of AI by farmers may be difficult as farmers may not possess the required skills to use AI in their fields. But, training programmes can be conducted to educate farmers about AI implementation in their fields. The adoption of AI depends on technical and regulatory norms. There are hurdles in the research and application of AI because of limited access to data, low awareness for adoption, and limited collaborative approach. The FPIs have different kinds of infrastructure bottlenecks. Cold storage facilities now available are mostly for single commodities like potatoes, oranges, apples, grapes, pomegranates, flowers *etc*, which result in poor capacity utilization. Without a strong and dependable cold storage facility, the FPIs based mostly on perishable products cannot survive and grow. There is a lack of technology in FPIs to utilize by-products in the primary processing stage of agri products. There is a need to create a coaction between production, processing, promotion and policy framework to develop linkages within the FPIs.

CONCLUSION

The use of AI in FPIs has increased production, improved quality, and reduced wastage. Sorting, grading, and cutting vegetables and fruits that required manual labour, all of these activities are replaced by automation. India has been in the forefront in terms of technological development. There are persistent efforts to modernize not only FPIs but also the agricultural sector. The Government is encouraging collaborations of all kinds for effective adoption of AI in the food industry. Though AI has revolutionized the market economy, its adoption in the FPIs is in its infant stage, so there will be a gradual absorption of AI tools in the FPIs of India. A McKinsey report has stated food wastage can be reduced by 127 billion US dollars by 2030 with the use of AI in FPIs. With investment in technological infrastructure and AI, there are opportunities to set up food tech startups. The FPI in India will undergo a transition with the use of AI technologies such as robotics and sensors, which help in sorting, processing, and packaging and save operational costs. This can be possible through adequate investment in AI and training in the implementation of AI tools. With the use of AI, it is possible to attain sustainable food processing, resulting in low carbon footprint and waste reduction and provide safe and healthy processed food products to all. The Government has to initiate private partnerships, encourage innovation through research and development, and apply a collaborative approach to support AI implementation in FPIs.

REFERENCES

[1]   Food and Drug Administration (FDA), United States: Economic Research Service of the United States Drug Administration, 1990. Available from: https://www.fda.gov/

[2]   The State of Food and Agriculture (FAO), Rome: Food and Agriculture Organisation, 1997. Available

from: https://www.fao.org/home/en

[3]   Government of India, Database of the Ministry of Food Processing Industries [MOFPIs], New Delhi: Ministry of Food Processing Industries, 2005. Available from: https://www.mofpi.gov.in/

[4]   Government of United Kingdom, Safety and hygiene publications, London: Food Standards Agency(FSA), 2002. Available from: https://www.food.gov.uk/

[5]   Annual Report (2022-23), Ministry of Food Processing Industry (MOFPI), Government of India, New Delhi, Available from: https://www.mofpi.gov.in/

[6]   Baldwin JR, Sabourin D. Enhancing food safety and productivity: technology use in the Canadian food processing industry. Soc Sci Res Netw 2002; (168): 1205-9153.

[7]   NITI AAYOG Annual Report, Government of India, 2018, 19. Available from: https://www.niti.gov.in/sites/default/files/2019-11/AnnualReport2019.pdf

[8]   IUFoST Scientific Information Bulletin (SIB). Recent Advances of Artificial Intelligence Applications in Food Industry; 2020. Available from: https://iufost.org/sites/default/files/documents/sibs/Artificial-Intelligence-Applications-in-Food.pdf

[9]   Zhu L, Spachos P, Pensini E, Plataniotis KN. Deep learning and machine vision for food processing: a survey. Curr Res Food Sci 2021; 233-49.
[http://dx.doi.org/10.1016/j.crfs.2021.03.009]

[10]   Talwar S. Artificial intelligence in the food processing industry in india; invest india, 2021 Available from: https://www.investindia.gov.in/team-india-blogs/artificial-intelligence-food-processing-in-ustry-india

[11]   Mavani N, Yuh L, Hashim H, *et al.* Fuzzy mamdani based user-friendly interface for food preservatives determination. Food Bioprod Process 2021; 126.
[http://dx.doi.org/10.1016/j.fbp.2021.01.012]

[12]   Romanello R, Veglio V. Industry 4.0 in food processing: drivers, challenges and outcomes. Br Food J 2022; 124(13): 375-90.
[http://dx.doi.org/10.1108/BFJ-09-2021-1056]

[13]   Food Future Foundation. Food Vision Report-2030. Available from: https://face-cii.in/w--content/uploads/2022/12/Food-Vision-Report-2030.pdf

[14]   Srivastava S. Food automation – how ai and robotics are transforming the future of the industry. 2024. Available from: https://nrai.org/food-automation-how-ai-and-robotics-are-transforming-the-future-of-the-industry/

[15]   Leo Kumar SP. Knowledge-based expert system in manufacturing planning. State-of-the-art review. Int J Prod Res 2019; 57(15–16): 4766-90.
[http://dx.doi.org/10.1080/00207543.2018.1424372]

[16]   Szturo K, Szczypinski PM. Ontology based expert system for barley grain classification. Signal Process-Algorithms, Archit, Arrang Appl Conf Proc (SPA). 360-4.
[http://dx.doi.org/10.23919/SPA.2017.8166893]

[17]   Sipos A. A knowledge-based system as a sustainable software application for the supervision and intelligent control of an alcoholic fermentation process. Sustainability (Basel) 2020; 12(23): 10205.
[http://dx.doi.org/10.3390/su122310205]

[18]   Suciu I, Ndiaye A, Baudrit C, *et al.* A digital learning tool based on models and simulators for food engineering (MESTRAL). J Food Eng 2020; 293.
[http://dx.doi.org/10.1016/j.jfoodeng.2020.110375]

[19]   Butler KT, Davies DW, Cartwright H, Isayev O, Walsh A. Machine learning for molecular and materials science. Nature 2018; 559(7715): 547-55.
[http://dx.doi.org/10.1038/s41586-018-0337-2] [PMID: 30046072]

[20]   Carleo G, Cirac I, Cranmer K, *et al.* Machine learning and the physical sciences. Rev Mod Phys 2019; 91(4): 045002.
[http://dx.doi.org/10.1103/RevModPhys.91.045002]

[21]   Li B, Lin Y, Yu W, *et al.* Application of mechanistic modelling and machine learning for cream cheese fermentation pH prediction. J Chem Technol Biotechnol 2020; 6517.
[http://dx.doi.org/10. 1002/ jctb]

[22]   Yan J, Guo X, Duan S, *et al.* Electronic nose feature extraction methods: a review. Sensors (Basel) 2015; 15(11): 27804-31.
[http://dx.doi.org/10. 3390/s1511 27804] [PMID: 26540056]

[23]   Baietto M, Wilson AD. Electronic-nose applications for fruit identification, ripeness and quality grading. Sensors (Switzerland). 2015; 15: pp. (1)899-931.
[http://dx.doi.org/10.3390/s150100899]

[24]   Wojnowski W, Majchrzak T, Dymerski T, Gębicki J, Namieśnik J. Portable electronic nose based on electrochemical sensors for food quality assessment. Sensors (Basel) 2017; 17(12): 1-14.
[http://dx.doi.org/10. 3390/ s1712 2715] [PMID: 29186754]

[25]   Gliszczyńska-Świgło A, Chmielewski J. Electronic nose as a tool for monitoring the authenticity of food. A review. Food Anal Methods 2017; 10(6): 1800-16.
[http://dx.doi.org/10.1007/s12161-016-0739-4]

[26]   Hoekstra S, Romme JJ, Argelo SM. Integral logistic structures: developing customer-oriented goods flow. 1992.

[27]   William D. An economic theory of technological change. Am Econ Rev 1969; 59(2): 18-28. Available from: https://www.jstor.org/stable/1823649

[28]   Yannis Bakos J, Chris F. Recent applications of economic theory in information technology research. Decis Support Syst 1992; 8(5): 365-86.
[http://dx.doi.org/10.1016/0167-9236(92)90024-J]

[29]   McCarthy J, Minsky M L. A proposal for the dartmouth summer research project on artificial intelligence. AI Mag 2006; 27(4): 12.
[http://dx.doi.org/10.1609/aimag.v27i4.1904]

[30]   Wiederhold G, McCarthy J, Samuel A. Pioneer in machine learning. IBM J Res Develop 1992; 36: 329-31.
[http://dx.doi.org/10.1147/rd.363.0329]

[31]   Pensinia E, Plataniotisb KN. Deep learning and machine vision for food processing: A survey. 2021. Available from: https://arxiv.org/pdf/2103.16106

[32]   Ardiansah I, Efatmi F, Mardawati E. Feasibility testing of a household industry food production certificate using an expert system with forward chaining method. J Inform Frequency 2020; 5(2): 137-44.
[http://dx.doi.org/10.15575/join.v5i2.579]

[33]   Yan J, Guo X, Duan S, *et al.* Electronic nose feature extraction methods: a review. Sensors (Switzerland) 2015;15(11):27804–27831.
[http://dx.doi.org/10.3390/s151127804]

[34]   NITI AAYOG Annual Report, Government of India, 2018-19, Available from: https://www.niti.gov.in/sites/default/files/2019-11/AnnualReport2019.pdf

[35]   Filter M, Appel B, Buschulte A. Expert systems for food safety. Curr Opin Food Sci 2016; 6: 61-5.
[http://dx.doi.org/10.1016/j.cofs.2016.01.004]

[36]   Annual Report, Ministry of Food Processing Industry (MOFPI), Government of India, New Delhi, 2022-23. Available from: https://www.mofpi.gov.in/

[37]   Government of India, Database of the Ministry of Food Processing Industries [MOFPIs] (2005), New Delhi: Ministry of Food Processing Industries, Available from: https://www.mofpi.gov.in/

[38]   Food Future Foundation 2022; Food Vision Report-2030. Available from: https://face-cii.in/w--content/uploads/2022/12/Food-Vision-Report-2030.pdf.

[39]   Mavani Nidhi, Mohd Ali Jarinah, Othman . Application of artificial intelligence in food industry—a guideline.   Food   Eng   Rev   2022;   14   Available   from: https://www.researchgate.net/publication/353777391_Application_of_Artificial_Intelligence_in_Food _Industry-a_Guideline/citation/download
[http://dx.doi.org/10.1007/s12393-021-09290-z]

[40]   Ministry of Food Processing Industry(MOFPI), Annual Report. Government of India 2024. Available from: https://www.mofpi.gov.in/

[41]   Borana J, Jodhpur NU. Borana J, Jodhpur NU. Applications of artificial intelligence & associated technologies. Proc Int Conf Emerg Technol Eng, Biomed, Manage Sci (ETEBMS) 2016. Available from: https://www.semanticscholar.org/paper/Applications-of-Artificial-Intelligence-%26-Borana/d5b061e6565ce421b4b0b7d56296e882085dc308

[42]   Choudhary A, Sood M, Singh J, *et al.* Artificial intelligence and its applications in the food The Pharma.   Innov   J   2023;   SP-12(7):   1351-5.   Available   from: https://www.thepharmajournal.com/archives/2023/vol12issue7S/PartP/S-12-7-154-165.pdf

[43]   Sanaeifar A, Zaki Dizaji H, Jafari A, *et al.* Early detection of contamination and defect in foodstuffs by electronic nose: a review. Trac - Trends Anal Chem 2017; 97: 257-71.
[http://dx.doi.org/10.1016/j.trac.2017.09.014] [http://dx.doi.org/10.1016/j.trac.2017.09.014]

[44]   Mohamed R R, Taacob R, Mohamed MA. Data mining techniques in food safety. Int J Adv Trends Comput Sci Eng 2015; 9(1.1): 379-84.

[45]   Mohamed R R, Taacob R, Mohamed MA, *et al.* Data mining techniques in food safety. International Journal of Advance Trends in Computer Science and Engineering, 2015, 9(1.1): 379-384.

CHAPTER 2

Sustainable Water Management Strategies

Tintu Vijayan[1,*], Jayanthi Ethiraj[1], Beldona Visweswara[1], Tharun Darur[1], Dudekula Sanjay[1] and **Muchamari Vishnu Vardhan[1]**

[1] *Department of CSE, Presidency University, Bangalore, India*

Abstract: Water resource management faces increasing challenges due to population growth, urbanization, climate change, and pollution—factors that threaten its ability to support life, ecosystems, and socioeconomic development. This chapter explores the potential of Large Language Models (LLMs), particularly GPT-4, to transform practices in water resource management. Since Large Language Models (LLMs) excel at processing extensive textual data and deriving insights, they hold significant potential for guiding decision-making in highly complex scenarios. This chapter demonstrates some recent research and applications in the domain of LLMs for efficiency improvement in water resource management, advancing predictive modelling, and supporting decision-making. Moreover, case studies on flood forecasting, water quality monitoring, and agricultural water management explain the practical use of LLMs in these aspects. Further, this chapter will highlight challenges associated with data quality, computational resources, and ethical considerations. Looking ahead, some critical enablers of the future in LLMs related to water management discuss developments in artificial intelligence, integration with technologies like IoT and blockchain, and supportive policy frameworks.

Keywords: Green infrastructure, Integrated water resources management, Rainwater harvesting, Water Conservation, Water efficiency, Water reuse and recycling.

INTRODUCTION

Water is a significant resource fundamental to life, ecosystems, and socio-economic development worldwide. Freshwater resources continue to be threatened by the growing populations, urbanization, and other impacts of climate change supported by other correlated forms of pollution. This calls for vision-related sustainable water management strategies using state-of-the-art available utilities and scientific breakthroughs [1]. One such application gaining promi-

---

* **Corresponding author Tintu Vijayan:** Department of CSE, Presidency University, Bangalore, India; E-mail: tintuidhaya@gmail.com

Raghavendra M. Devadas, Vani Hiremani, Praveen Gujjar Jagannath, Lubna Ambreen & Harold Andrew Patrick (Eds.)

nence is the application of large language models in enhancing the effectiveness of water management practices. LLMs, such as GPT-4, leverage advanced artificial intelligence and to handle vast textual data to drive inference and provide impetus to decision-making processes in complicated scenarios. These models have increased their adoption in most usage areas at a rapid rate in many domains, such as analysis and interpretation, trend prediction, and resource allocation optimization [2]. The quantity and quality of freshwater resources are said to be under increasing threat due to growing populations, urbanization, impacts of climate change, and challenges posed by pollution. This chapter identifies the potential of Large Language Models (LLMs) to drive transformational change toward more sustainable water management. Synthesizing the knowledge from extant contemporary research and its practical applications displays how much the LLMs will actually help to drive immense improvements in increasing efficiency within water resources management, strengthening predictive modeling capabilities *via* data-driven intelligence, and enhancing informed decision-making [3]. What is also critically reflected upon, of course, are challenges that have to be faced and such ethical considerations in the setup and deployment of LLMs in the context of water management. Discussion on these issues was based on peer-reviewed literature and empirical studies about the current status and prospects of LLMs as integrated parts of sustainable water management strategies. By elaborating on these developments, this chapter contributes to the ongoing discourse on leveraging technology to effectively address some of the pressing global water challenges. LLMs have been employed to optimize water distribution networks by analyzing vast amounts of data to identify inefficiencies and suggest improvements. A case in point is cities facing water scarcity, where LLMs can inform the development of strategies for both effective and equitable water distribution by analyzing consumption patterns, weather forecasts, and infrastructural data. This not only supports a stable water supply but also reduces water loss and operational costs. One of the most impressive aspects, in this case, is predictive modeling. By integrating climate models with hydrological data, these models can project future water availability, foresee drought conditions, and predict flood events accurately. For instance, in areas that experience seasonal flooding, LLMs can combine basic historical weather data with real-time sensor input to provide early warnings that allow for community preparation and mitigation of potential damages [4]. Furthermore, this enhances informed decision-making by helping to provide a detailed analysis of environmental policies alongside their possible impacts. LLMs are used to simulate scenarios in which the consequences of alternative regulatory strategies can be compared for resolving ecological sustainability and economic growth. It is their ability to process and analyze complex datasets that make these models invaluable for developing and implementing policies aimed at effective water management.

The chapter critically engages with the existing challenges and ethical considerations linked to the deployment of LLMs within water management contexts. This would include concerns about data privacy, clarity in AI decision-making processes, and biases potentially conveyed through data into the outcome. LLM applications should be designed in ways that clearly conform to ethical standards and promote fair access to water resources on the part of the user [5]. The paper discusses, with reference to peer-reviewed literature and empirical studies, the current state and future prospects of LLMs as integrative parts within sustainable water management strategies. The chapter adds to the ongoing discourse on how technology can be harnessed effectively to counter some of the urgent global water challenges by elaborating on these developments. Table **1** shows the Comparison of Sustainable Water Management Strategies Before and After the Implementation of Large Language Models (LLMs).

Table 1. Comparison of sustainable water management strategies before and after implementation of large language models (LLMs).

Parameter	Before LLM Implementation	After LLM Implementation
Data Processing Efficiency	Manual data collection and processing were time-consuming and error-prone.	Automated data analysis and processing reduced processing time significantly.
Predictive Accuracy	Predictions based on simplified models with moderate accuracy.	Enhanced predictive models improved accuracy in water availability forecasts.
Stakeholder Engagement	Limited stakeholder involvement due to communication barriers.	Increased stakeholder engagement through interactive decision support systems.
Resource Allocation Efficiency	Resource allocation decisions were based on historical data and projections.	Optimized resource allocation using real-time data and scenario simulations.
Response Time to Water Crises	Delayed response times due to manual crisis assessment and decision-making.	Rapid response is enabled by early warning systems and real-time data analytics.
Policy Formulation Effectiveness	Policy decisions are based on limited data insights and outdated models.	Informed policy formulation supported by comprehensive data-driven analyses.
Environmental Impact Assessment	Environmental impacts assessed using traditional methodologies.	Enhanced environmental impact assessments integrating predictive analytics.

CASE STUDIES AND APPLICATIONS

This section details how several such low-level models have been used as described and clearly demonstrates how they relate to real-world issues in the management of water. It demonstrates, therefore, the practical utility and consequences of using them. In flood-prone areas, LLMs have been used by examining historic weather datasets, topographical data, and live sensor data to predict the events that cause floods. In flood-prone areas, Low-Level Models (LLMs) have been effectively utilized by examining historic weather datasets, topographical data, and live sensor data to predict the events that cause floods. By integrating diverse sources of data, such models can provide accurate predictions of flood events, allowing for timely and effective responses. For instance, historical weather data can reveal patterns and trends in precipitation that contribute to flooding. Topographical data helps in understanding the landscape and how water might flow and accumulate in different areas. Live sensor data, including river levels, soil moisture, and real-time weather conditions, provides up-to-date information that is crucial for immediate flood risk assessment.

These models have been employed in various real-world scenarios to enhance flood preparedness and response strategies. For example, in regions like the Mississippi River Basin in the United States, LLMs have been used to predict flood events and mitigate damage. Authorities can issue early warnings, plan evacuations, and mobilize resources more effectively due to the insights provided by these models. In urban areas, such as Jakarta, Indonesia, where flooding is a recurring problem, the integration of LLMs with city planning and infrastructure development has shown promising results. These models help in designing better drainage systems and implementing zoning laws that reduce flood risks.

Moreover, the application of LLMs is not limited to flood prediction alone. They are also used in managing water resources by predicting droughts and optimizing irrigation schedules in agricultural areas. This ensures that water usage is efficient and sustainable, ultimately supporting food security and reducing the economic impact of water shortages.

Through these case studies, it becomes evident that LLMs play a crucial role in addressing water management challenges. Their ability to process and analyze large volumes of data from various sources enables decision-makers to predict, prepare for, and respond to water-related issues with greater precision and effectiveness.

Flood Forecasting and Control

Flood forecasting and control are critical for mitigating the devastating impacts of floods. Advanced technologies, such as remote sensing and Geographic Information Systems (GIS), play a pivotal role in these processes. Remote sensing provides real-time data on rainfall, river levels, and soil moisture, enabling accurate flood predictions. GIS integrates this data with topographical and historical flood information to model flood scenarios and predict affected areas. Early warning systems, leveraging these technologies, can alert communities and authorities, allowing timely evacuations and preparations. Structural measures like dams, levees, and retention basins are combined with non-structural approaches such as land-use planning and public awareness campaigns. Together, these strategies enhance resilience, reduce economic losses, and save lives by providing a comprehensive approach to flood management and response [6]. In flood-prone areas, LLMs have been used by examining historic weather datasets, topographical data, and live sensor data to predict the events that cause floods. The timely and accurate predictions of these models have enabled authorities to take proactive measures that reduce the sufferings of communities and infrastructures from the flood. Researchers from the Netherlands used LLMs based on data from weather stations, river gauges, and satellite imaging to improve flood prediction accuracy. The model engages in real-time prediction analysis of historical flood data and precipitation forecasts, thus enhancing the accuracy of its predictions. This helped to give notice of a flood early enough and turn on the necessary practices when dealing with disasters, significantly reducing adverse flooding effects on an urban and rural scale [7].

Researchers from the Netherlands have made significant advancements in flood prediction by leveraging LLMs based on data from weather stations, river gauges, and satellite imaging. These models engage in real-time prediction analysis by integrating historical flood data and precipitation forecasts, thereby enhancing the accuracy of their predictions. For instance, by analyzing patterns in past flood events and correlating them with current weather conditions, LLMs can provide early warnings of potential flooding. This capability is crucial for disaster preparedness and response, allowing authorities to implement necessary measures well in advance [8].

In urban areas, early flood warnings enable city planners and emergency services to mobilize resources, evacuate vulnerable populations, and protect critical infrastructure. For example, flood barriers can be erected, drainage systems can be optimized, and emergency shelters can be prepared. This proactive approach significantly mitigates the impact of floods on urban populations, reducing both human suffering and economic losses. In rural areas, where communities may rely heavily on agriculture, accurate flood predictions help safeguard livelihoods. Farmers can receive timely alerts to move livestock, secure equipment, and take other preventive measures to protect their crops from flood damage. Additionally, early warnings enable rural communities to prepare for potential disruptions in transportation and supply chains, ensuring that they can maintain access to essential goods and services during flood events. The integration of LLMs with satellite imaging also offers a broader perspective on flood dynamics. Satellite data provides real-time information on precipitation, river levels, and soil moisture content across large geographical areas. This comprehensive view allows LLMs to identify regions at risk of flooding with greater precision, enhancing the overall effectiveness of flood prediction and management strategies.

The application of LLMs in flood forecasting has also facilitated better coordination between different agencies and stakeholders involved in disaster management. By providing a centralized platform for data analysis and prediction, LLMs enable seamless communication and collaboration among meteorological departments, emergency services, and local governments. This coordinated effort ensures a more efficient and effective response to flood threats. Furthermore, the success of LLM-based flood forecasting systems in the Netherlands has inspired similar initiatives in other parts of the world. For instance, countries with high flood risk, such as Bangladesh and India, are exploring the use of LLMs to enhance their flood prediction capabilities [9]. By adapting the models to local conditions and incorporating region-specific data, these countries aim to improve their resilience to flooding and reduce the associated human and economic costs.

Water Quality Monitoring

Water quality monitoring is essential for ensuring the safety and health of aquatic ecosystems and human communities. It involves the systematic collection and analysis of water samples to evaluate physical, chemical, and biological parameters. Key indicators include pH, dissolved oxygen, turbidity, temperature, and the presence of contaminants such as heavy metals and pathogens. Advanced techniques like remote sensing, satellite imagery, and GIS are increasingly used to assess and predict water quality over large areas. These tools facilitate real-time data collection and analysis, enabling rapid response to pollution events. Continuous monitoring helps in the early detection of changes in water quality, guiding conservation efforts, regulatory compliance, and public health initiatives. Effective water quality management requires collaboration among scientists, policymakers, and stakeholders to maintain and improve water resources sustainably [10].

LMs have been constructed to monitor water quality by processing data from multiple sensors and sources like this, including remote sensing imagery and environmental reports. Such models can recognize anomalies and potential pollution sources soon enough, allowing responsive actions to limit their consequences [11]. In China, an LLM-based system for real-time water quality monitoring was implemented over the Yangtze River. The detection system used sensors measuring several water quality parameters, such as pH levels, turbidity, and chemical contaminations. Early alerts were raised to the government with the help of the already developed trend prediction of pollution and confusion detection of anomalies for taking necessary action on pollution sources, which should be crucial for water quality. The approach was practical, and such systems were efficient for better water safety and meeting the required standards of the regulators.

In China, an LLM-based system for real-time water quality monitoring was implemented over the Yangtze River. The detection system used sensors measuring several water quality parameters, such as pH levels, turbidity, and chemical contaminations. Early alerts were raised to the government with the help of the already developed trend prediction of pollution and confusion detection of anomalies, enabling authorities to take necessary actions on pollution sources. This approach was crucial for maintaining water quality, ensuring safety, and meeting regulatory standards [12].

Agricultural Water Management

Agricultural water management involves the strategic planning and control of water resources to enhance crop production and ensure sustainability. Effective management practices include irrigation scheduling, which optimizes water use by matching supply with crop needs, and the implementation of efficient irrigation systems like drip or sprinkler irrigation that minimize water loss. Additionally, soil moisture monitoring and the use of drought-resistant crop varieties play critical roles in conserving water. Integrating remote sensing and GIS technologies enables precise monitoring and management of water resources, allowing farmers to make informed decisions based on real-time data. These practices not only improve water use efficiency but also mitigate the impacts of water scarcity, contributing to food security and environmental sustainability [13]. Proper agricultural water management is essential for adapting to climate change and maintaining agricultural productivity in the face of increasing water demands and changing precipitation patterns. They have optimized irrigation practices by analyzing soil moisture, weather forecasts, and crop requirements; using water efficiently to improve yields helps reduce wastage in agricultural fields—a mainstay in agriculture [14]. An LLM-based input decision support system was developed for the irrigation management of a drought-prone area in the Maharashtra state of India. The real-time data included soil moisture status, local weather forecasts, and crop growth stages to project optimum irrigation schedules. This has maximally reduced water usage by 20% and amplified the crop by 15%. This shows the vitality of LLMs in realizing greater agricultural sustainability and resilience [15].

The LLM-based system in Maharashtra highlights how advanced technology can revolutionize traditional agricultural practices. By continuously monitoring soil moisture levels through sensors placed in the fields, the system provides precise data on the water needs of crops. This real-time information is then cross-referenced with weather forecasts, which predict upcoming rainfall and temperature conditions, ensuring that irrigation is scheduled only when necessary. This targeted approach not only conserves water but also ensures that crops receive the optimal amount of moisture for healthy growth.

In addition to soil moisture and weather data, the system takes into account the specific growth stages of crops. Different stages of crop development require varying amounts of water, and over-irrigation at certain stages can be as detrimental as under-irrigation. By tailoring irrigation schedules to the precise needs of crops at each growth stage, the LLM-based system maximizes water use efficiency and enhances crop productivity. The implementation of this system has had a profound impact on the agricultural landscape in Maharashtra. Farmers have reported a significant reduction in water usage, which is critical in a drought-prone area where water resources are scarce. The reduction of water usage by 20% not only conserves this vital resource but also translates into cost savings for farmers, who spend less on water procurement and pumping. Moreover, the 15% increase in crop yields demonstrates the system's effectiveness in enhancing agricultural productivity [16]. Higher yields mean more food production, contributing to food security and providing economic benefits to farmers. This increase in productivity also supports the livelihoods of farming communities, making them more resilient to the challenges posed by climate change and water scarcity. The success of the LLM-based irrigation system in Maharashtra has broader implications for agricultural practices globally. In regions facing similar challenges of water scarcity and drought, such systems can be adapted and implemented to improve water management and crop productivity. This approach aligns with the goals of sustainable agriculture, which seeks to balance the need for increased food production with the conservation of natural resources.

Furthermore, the use of LLMs in irrigation management can contribute to the broader goal of climate-smart agriculture. Efficient water use reduces the energy required for irrigation, thereby lowering greenhouse gas emissions associated with agricultural practices. This is particularly important in the context of global efforts to mitigate climate change and reduce the carbon footprint of farming [17]. The deployment of LLMs in irrigation management also underscores the importance of integrating technology with traditional farming knowledge. By combining advanced data analytics with the experience and expertise of local farmers, the system can be fine-tuned to address specific regional challenges and conditions. This collaborative approach ensures that technological solutions are practical, effective, and sustainable in the long term [18].

These case studies demonstrate how actual applications of LLMs work toward improving sustainable water management strategies, as in Fig. (1). LLMs could efficiently enhance the effectiveness and practices of water management by considering the potential capacities involving data analysis, decision support, and knowledge dissemination for practice improvement of water management toward sustainability and resilience in the challenge of continuously increasing environmental adversity [19].

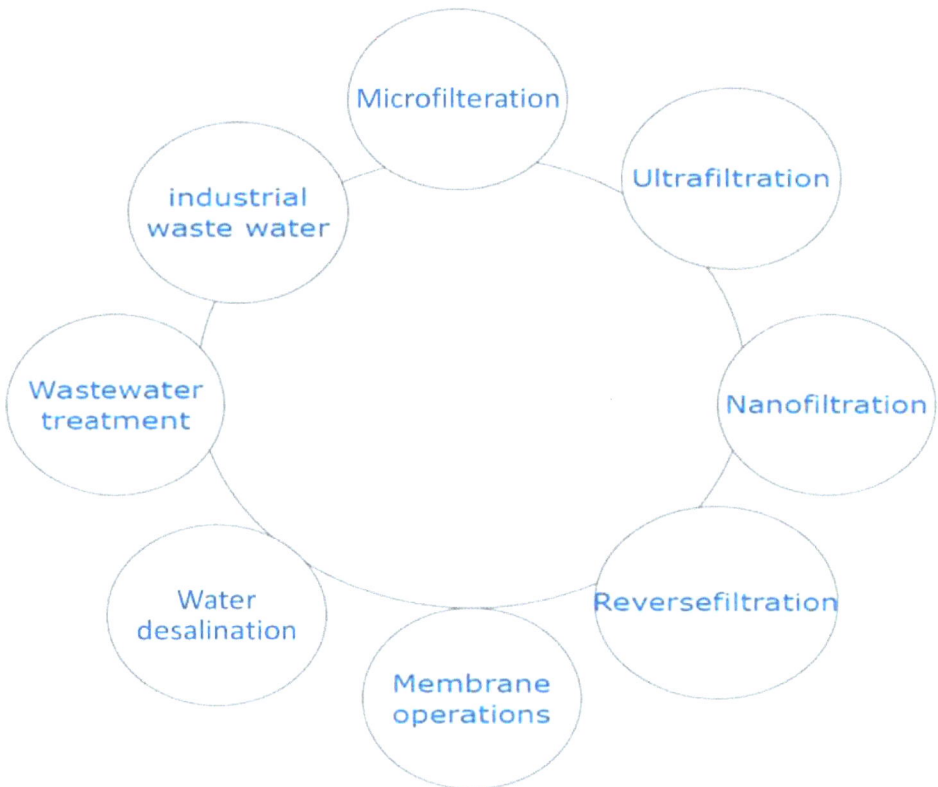

Fig. (1). Membrane technology for sustainable water resources management.

CHALLENGES AND LIMITATIONS

Methods such as water recycling, desalination, catchment management, water use efficiency, groundwater utilization, and surface water management have been proposed as comprehensive approaches to enhancing resilience and sustainability in water systems Nonetheless, they are also associated with major challenges and limitations.

For instance, desalination is often energy-consuming and expensive to boot, with environmental concerns about brine disposal. Reuse of water necessitates appropriate technology and public acceptance, which is often plagued by misconceptions regarding its safety and quality. Groundwater is being over-extracted and is prone to contamination. Surface water, on the other hand, relies upon good governance of catchment and climate adaptability. Similarly, the improvement in the efficiency of water use requires behavioral changes and modern irrigation systems, as well as financial investments, all of which can be limiting in resource-poor settings.

These require coordinated policy intervention, technological innovation, stakeholder engagement, and mechanisms of equable resource distribution. Fig. (2) below represents the multilevel integration that will help resolve complex water management challenges in a sustainable manner.

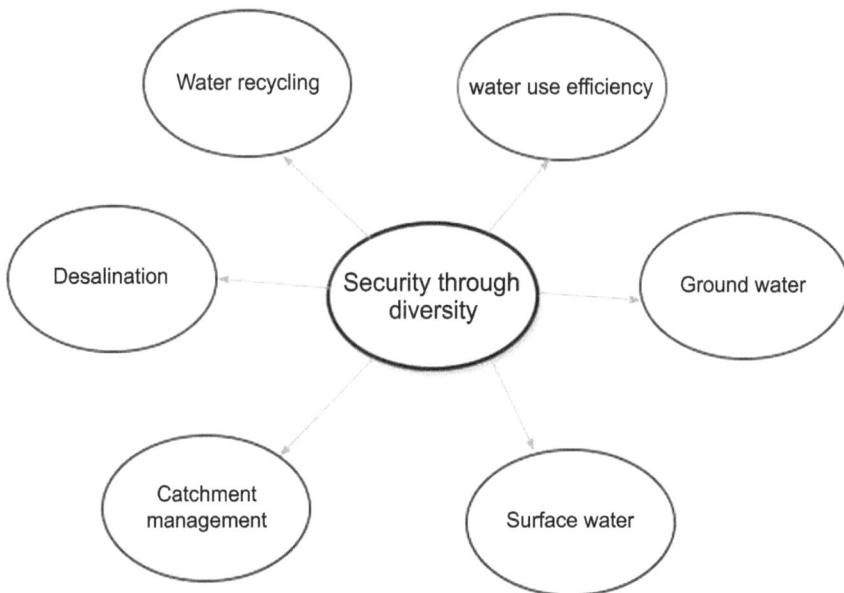

Fig. (2). Security through diversity in sustainable water management.

Data Quality and Availability

In sustainable water resource management, Large Language Models (LLMs) hold significant potential—primarily due to their ability to leverage high-quality and accessible data. However, several challenges remain.

Inconsistent and Incomplete Data

In most countries, especially in the developing world, data on water resources are either inconsistent or incomplete. Factors to blame could include a small number of monitoring structures, lack of data collection standardization, and historical neglect toward the problem of data maintenance. If data are inconsistent, then it reflects the unreliability of predictions and models; thus, no effective strategy for water management can be obtained.

Data Sparsity

Problems in data coverage could be significant in well-covered regions because of difficulties in geographically remote areas and areas that are difficult to access. Prominent challenges include sparse data collection points and faults or gaps in the source data upon which LLMs base their analyses and predictions.

Outdated Data

In periods of rapid environmental change, historical data may become outdated very quickly. Climate change and land use alterations are two major drivers reshaping water resource dynamics in ways that older datasets often fail to capture. Moreover, there is a risk that LLMs, by becoming increasingly detached from the limitations of their input data, may produce insights and recommendations that are not only inaccurate but potentially harmful—a technological shifting of the goalposts.

Computational Resources

The LLMs require giant computational resources that, in some cases, might give an apparatus not to be used.

High Power of Computation

This characterizes training and running the computations in LLMs as very computationally intensive tasks for the duty to consume significant amounts of energy, raising costs. For agencies operating on slender budgetary provisions or in regions where computational facilities and infrastructures are not at a high level, this disadvantage can be catastrophic.

Accessibility Issues

The required infrastructure for supporting LLMs, like high-performance computer clusters and cloud computing, is likely inaccessible to everyone. Developing countries, in particular, may have difficulty acquiring the necessary technology and skills to effectively implement LLMs in water.

Ethical and Privacy Issues

Several human ethical and privacy concerns to be considered in the use of LLMs for water management include:

Data Privacy

Large Language Models often have to be burdened with vast troves of data, which, in certain situations, might contain sensitive or personal information. This gift, therefore, puts the responsibility of the researcher or the engineer to handle the data in ways that fit prescribed privacy regulations. Unauthorized access or misuse of data could lead to serious ethical and legal consequences stemming from such breaches

Bias and Fairness

The biases embedded within the data are, thus, in the case of water management, biased decisions taken at the governmental level to affect a different community and region. Ensuring that deploying these models leads to fairness and equity, not reinforcing inversion, is fundamental.

Interpretability and Transparency

An essential class of issues about LLMs is their interpretability and transparency.

Nature of Black Box

Decision-making in LLMs is often described as operating within a 'black box,' and the lack of transparency associated with this model undermines both user trust and, more critically, adoption—especially in high-stakes domains such as water management, where reliability is essential.

Explainability

Methodologies that describe how LLMs reach their predictions are under ongoing development. Improving the interpretability of this class of models, therefore, opens the potential for building trust in them for use and, as a result, for their application to water management policies.

FUTURE DIRECTIONS

The future of remote sensing and GIS applications in agriculture promises substantial advancements. Emerging technologies, such as high-resolution satellite imagery, Unmanned Aerial Vehicles (UAVs), and advanced machine learning algorithms, are poised to enhance precision farming practices. These innovations will enable more accurate monitoring of crop health, soil moisture, and pest infestations, leading to improved decision-making and resource management. Additionally, the integration of Internet of Things (IoT) devices with GIS platforms is expected to provide real-time data, further optimizing agricultural practices. The development of user-friendly, accessible software will empower farmers globally, fostering sustainable agricultural practices and ensuring food security. As these technologies evolve, interdisciplinary collaboration and continuous innovation will be essential to address the challenges of climate change, population growth, and resource scarcity. Large language models represent the future of sustainable water management applications, with novel benchmarks and implementations underway [20]. All analyses to improve the same facilities and, at the same time, taking into consideration the very few limitations that are found will pave the way for improved strategies on the sustainable grounds of water resources management. The potential of LLMs in water management lies in their ability to process and analyze vast amounts of data from diverse sources, including meteorological reports, hydrological models, sensor networks, and satellite imagery. This capability allows for more accurate predictions and better decision-making processes, which are essential for managing water resources effectively in the face of growing challenges such as climate change, population growth, and urbanization.

For instance, LLMs can be used to develop more sophisticated models for predicting water availability and demand, taking into account factors such as seasonal variations, long-term climate trends, and changes in land use. These models can help water managers allocate resources more efficiently, ensuring that water is available where and when it is needed most. Additionally, LLMs can aid in the optimization of water distribution networks, reducing losses and improving the reliability of supply systems.

In the realm of water quality management, LLMs can be employed to monitor and predict the occurrence of pollutants and contaminants. By analyzing data from water quality sensors and integrating it with information on industrial activities, agricultural practices, and weather conditions, these models can identify potential sources of pollution and predict their impacts on water bodies. This enables proactive measures to be taken to prevent or mitigate contamination, ensuring the safety and health of water resources.

Moreover, the adaptability of LLMs means they can be tailored to specific regional and local contexts, addressing unique challenges and leveraging local data and knowledge. This flexibility is crucial for developing solutions that are both effective and sustainable, meeting the needs of different communities and ecosystems. Despite their potential, it is important to recognize the limitations of LLMs in water management. These include issues related to data quality and availability, the need for significant computational resources, and the risk of algorithmic biases. Addressing these limitations requires ongoing research and development, as well as collaboration between technologists, water managers, policymakers, and local communities. To fully harness the capabilities of LLMs for sustainable water management, it is essential to invest in the development of robust data infrastructures, promote data sharing and interoperability, and ensure that models are transparent and interpretable. Additionally, there is a need to build capacity among water management professionals to understand and utilize these advanced tools effectively.

Advances in AI and Machine Learning

Making more significant advances in artificial intelligence and machine learning will ideally improve overall LLM performance in water management; empirical evidence suggests that the coupling of deep learning with hydrologic models can enhance prediction accuracy, and near real-time decision-making can be facilitated. Currently, methods are developed to recalibrate the algorithms; that is, the reducing state dimension of the algorithms becomes more data-driven, or the algorithms represent the models that become better calibrated with new data.

Interaction with Other Technologies

It opens up quite several opportunities for the use of more robust and secure technologies through the broader integration of the Internet of Things into water management systems coupled with blockchain technology. For instance, such technologies as IoT-enabled sensors can supply real-time data on water quality and quantity. At the same time, LLMs are in a position to analyze this to optimize resource allocation and reduction of risks [9]. Blockchain tech plays a significant role in materially contributing toward trusted, secure data for all stakeholders involved concerning water governance and management [2]. Future research will aim to check the synergies of the above technologies along with LLMs for an all-encompassing, adaptive, and sustainable approach to resolving water governance challenges.

Policy and Regulatory Environments

Effective policy frameworks and regulatory guidelines are essential, as they guide the responsible deployment of LLMs within water management. Further emphasizing the need for effective policies and frameworks, one study advocates for governance models that offer flexibility to accommodate technological advancements while minimizing compromises to environmental and societal interests [3]. Future directions will consider the development of strategies that will ensure data sharing, the exercise of ethical data use, and the involvement of stakeholders as a process of inclusive policies [4]. Through technology-based progress, harmonization of regulatory frameworks with technological advancements will place policymakers in the best position to harness the potential of LLMs for sustainable water management.

CONCLUSION

In conclusion, the large language model represents a new frontier in the redefinition and refinement of sustainable water management strategies; so, this power of ability in data analysis, decision support, and knowledge dissemination makes LLMs quite useful in transforming how water resources management can be performed. New studies have highlighted the effectiveness of LLMs in varied applications for water management. For instance, the importance of LLMs in recent years has been to deal with every model parameter model through an objective and robust parameter optimization process to provide a holistic increase in model prediction accuracy. In other words, significant opportunities come from the integration of large language models in sustaining water management practices for better environmental outcomes and the building of resilience in communities.

REFERENCES

[1]   Batarseh FA, Kulkarni A. AI for water. Computer 2023; 56(3): 109-13.
       [http://dx.doi.org/10.1109/MC.2022.3231142]

[2]   Xu B, Wen L, Li Z, *et al.* Unlocking the potential: benchmarking large language models in water engineering and research. arXiv preprint arXiv 2024.

[3]   Samuel DJ, Sermet MY, Mount J, Vald G, Cwiertny D, Demir I. Application of large language models in developing conversational agents for water quality education, communication and operations, 2024.

[4]   Kadiyala L, Mermer O, Samuel DJ, Sermet Y, Demir I. A comprehensive evaluation of multimodal large language models in hydrological applications, 2024.
       [http://dx.doi.org/10.31223/X5TQ37]

[5]   Dang Q, Konar M, Reimer JJ, Di Baldassarre G, Lin X, Zeng R. A theoretical model of water and trade. Adv Water Resour 2016; 89: 32-41.
       [http://dx.doi.org/10.1016/j.advwatres.2015.12.016]

[6]   De Moel H, Van Alphen J, Aerts JCJH. Flood maps in Europe – methods, availability and use. Nat Hazards Earth Syst Sci 2009; 9(2): 289-301.

[http://dx.doi.org/10.5194/nhess-9-289-2009]

[7]   Morante-Carballo F, Montalván-Burbano N, Arias-Hidalgo M, Domínguez-Granda L, Apolo-Masache B, Carrión-Mero P. Flood models: An exploratory analysis and research trends. Water 2022; 14(16): 2488.
[http://dx.doi.org/10.3390/w14162488]

[8]   Petersen-Perlman JD, Aguilar-Barajas I, Megdal SB. Drought and groundwater management: Interconnections, challenges, and policyresponses. Curr Opin Environ Sci Health 2022; 28: 100364.
[http://dx.doi.org/10.1016/j.coesh.2022.100364]

[9]   Hasanuzzaman M, Hossain S, Shil SK. Enhancing disaster management through AI-driven predictive analytics: improving preparedness and response. International Journal of Advanced Engineering Technologies and Innovations 2023; 1(01): 533-62.

[10]   Carstens D, Amer R. Spatio-temporal analysis of urban changes and surface water quality. J Hydrol (Amst) 2019; 569: 720-34.
[http://dx.doi.org/10.1016/j.jhydrol.2018.12.033]

[11]   Chauhan D, Bahad P, Jain JK. Sustainable AI: environmental implications, challenges, and opportunities. Explainable AI (XAI) Sustain Dev 2024; 1-5.

[12]   Dou F, Ye J, Yuan G, *et al.* Towards artificial general intelligence (AGI) in the internet of things (IoT): opportunities and challenges. arXiv preprint arXiv 2023.

[13]   Debbarma S, Beniwal D, Singh TC, Daniel GR. Drip fertigation in vegetable crops for higher crop productivity and resource use efficiency-a review. Chem Sci Rev Lett 2018; 7(28): 971-7.

[14]   Knox J, Hess T, Daccache A, Wheeler T. Climate change impacts on crop productivity in Africa and South Asia. Environ Res Lett 2012; 7(3): 034032.
[http://dx.doi.org/10.1088/1748-9326/7/3/034032]

[15]   Dias SN. A novel strategy to improve water productivity in rice cultivation: a case study from Sri Lanka. Dissertation, Technische Universität Dresden 2019.

[16]   Xing Y, Wang X. Precision agriculture and water conservation strategies for sustainable crop production in arid regions. Plants 2024; 13(22): 3184.
[http://dx.doi.org/10.3390/plants13223184] [PMID: 39599396]

[17]   Berardy A, Chester MV. Climate change vulnerability in the food, energy, and water nexus: concerns for agricultural production in Arizona and its urban export supply. Environ Res Lett 2017; 12(3): 035004.
[http://dx.doi.org/10.1088/1748-9326/aa5e6d]

[18]   Fuentes-Peñailillo F, Gutter K, Vega R, Silva GC. Transformative technologies in digital agriculture: Leveraging Internet of Things, remote sensing, and artificial intelligence for smart crop management. Journal of Sensor and Actuator Networks 2024; 13(4): 39.
[http://dx.doi.org/10.3390/jsan13040039]

[19]   Ali A, Hussain T, Tantashutikun N, Hussain N, Cocetta G. Application of smart techniques, internet of things and data mining for resource use efficient and sustainable crop production. Agriculture 2023; 13(2): 397.
[http://dx.doi.org/10.3390/agriculture13020397]

[20]   Triantafyllou A, Sarigiannidis P, Bibi S. Precision agriculture: A remote sensing monitoring system architecture. Information. 2019 Nov 9;10(11):348.

CHAPTER 3

Remote Sensing and GIS Applications in Agriculture

Tintu Vijayan[1,*], Indupuri Mohan Vamsi[1], Sreelatha[1] and **Jayanthi Ethiraj[1]**

[1] *Department of Computer Science and Engineering, Presidency University, Bangalore, India*

Abstract: Advanced technologies that underlie the seamless integration of Remote Sensing (RS), Geographic Information Systems (GIS), and Large Language Models (LLMs) have transformed modern agriculture. This chapter explores the synergistic effects of these technologies, demonstrating that their integration is truly disruptive in agriculture. RS technologies represent a source of fundamental data for crop health, soil conditions, and environmental changes through satellite and UAV imagery. GIS enhances this data by providing spatial analysis and mapping, which facilitates precision agriculture through variable input application and resource management. The introduction of LLMs, especially GPT-4-like models, adds a new dimension to agricultural data interpretation. LLMs can process huge volumes of unstructured data, from scientific literature to field reports, in order to arrive at the correct decisions related to crop management, pest control, and yield prediction. The chapter focuses on integrating RS, GIS, and LLMs methodologies and their applications in agriculture. Case studies for yield prediction and pest monitoring are examples of how feasible such initiatives are and promise improvement in productivity and sustainability in farming.

Keywords: Geographic information systems (GIS), Large language models (LLMs), Precision agriculture, Remote sensing (RS).

INTRODUCTION

Agriculture has recorded unprecedented growth in the past years because it has integrated with state-of-the-art technologies. Without RS and GIS, collection, analysis, and exploitation of data related to agriculture are impossible. Simultaneously, advancements in data interpretation and decision-making powered by Large Language Models have opened new avenues in agriculture. This chapter exemplifies how such technologies integrate to create disruptive effects in agriculture.

---

[*] **Corresponding author Tintu Vijayan:** Department of Computer Science and Engineering, Presidency University, Bangalore, India; E-mail: tintuidhaya@gmail.com

Raghavendra M. Devadas, Vani Hiremani, Praveen Gujjar Jagannath, Lubna Ambreen & Harold Andrew Patrick (Eds.)

Remote sensing is the process of acquiring information about an object or phenomenon without directly coming into contact with the object; this may be *via* satellite or aerial photographs [1]. RS is one such essential application in agriculture, wherein crop health status and yield estimation, pest and disease detection, and resource management are assessed. Satellite missions, like Landsat and Sentinel, provide a lot of data related to vegetation indices. Among them, NDVI is very important in the estimation of plant health and productivity [2].

The combination of RS and GIS has been very effective in addressing critical challenges to agriculture. For instance, the integration of satellite images with GIS would give one an accurate map of the crop growth stages to the extent of even pinpointing areas that require interventions. This synergy thus achieves better efficiency in agricultural operations for better yields while lessening environmental impacts.

LLMs, including OpenAI's GPT-3 and GPT-4, as shown in Fig. (**1**), represent remarkable achievements in AI. These models have been trained on vast textual data so that they can understand contexts and generate a human-like text. Domains related to natural language processing, translations, and information retrieval are a few of the large unfolding areas for LLM applications.

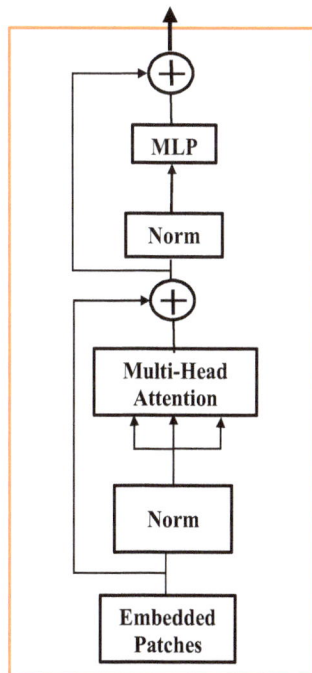

Fig. (1). Transformer encoder.

There are various ways in which LLMs can uniquely benefit farming by processing and extracting meaningful insights from large volumes of unstructured data ranging from research articles to field reports and sensor data. For example, LLMs have already been used to mine scientific literature that generates recent findings and recommendations relative to certain topics for farmers and researchers [3].

It is no sweat for LLMs to draw up detailed reports and reply in natural language to complex questions, making them ideal decision-support systems in agriculture. Their understanding and contextualizing ability make them quite fit for specially tailoring advice related to crop management, soil health, pest control, and all other very critical farming recommendations in this subject area.

It is estimated that LLMs would further increase the interpretation of the RS and GIS data analysis in detecting a pattern or correlation that otherwise would have been elusive to traditional methods. For example, LLMs can easily project crop yields from their past temporal satellite imagery data and even detect any incipient signs of stressors, such as pests or diseases. It is possible to combine such predictions with GIS and, therefore, allow farmers to map the spatial distribution of these threats and apply interventions in a site-specific manner [4].

Moreover, LLM-based data from heterogeneous sources, RS imaginary, GIS layers, and text research publications/field reports, can be integrated. Hence, data fusion becomes possible for detailed analysis of agricultural systems/crop dynamics with environmental interactions. For example, LLMs could consider all information that relates to soil properties and weather patterns to provide crop phenology in order to recommend the optimum time for sowing and harvesting a certain crop.

This kind of integration opens up several practical applications within precision agriculture. The LLMs are in a position to enhance the decision-supporting systems through dynamic recommendations from the RS and GIS data in real-time so that farmers can make informed decisions on irrigation, fertilization, and pest management for effective productivity and sustainability.

Agricultural Applications of Remote Sensing Technologies

Contemporary agriculture is simply impossible without remote sensing technologies providing a core source of data about crop conditions, soil conditions, and environmental changes. It considers the following subjects: different types of remote sensing, main sensors and platforms, data acquisition, and preprocessing techniques.

There are three types of remote sensing, namely satellite, aerial, and Unmanned Aerial Vehicles (UAVs).

Satellite Remote Sensing

Satellite remote sensing involves satellites that orbit the Earth, equipped with sensors capturing electromagnetic radiation in different wavelengths. These sensors can, therefore, be ideal for monitoring large agricultural areas as a result of their functionality that allows large scale coverage and quite frequent visits.

• Multispectral and Hyperspectral Imaging: Multispectral sensors perceive information in discrete wavelength bands, while hyperspectral ones obtain data in hundreds of narrow contiguous bands. They find applications in monitoring vegetation health, classification of crops, and soil analysis [5].
• Radar Sensors: In synthetic aperture radar, microwave signals pass through clouds, generating information related to soil moisture, crop structure, and terrain features.

Aerial Remote Sensing

Aerial remote sensing would use manned aircraft to provide high-resolution images over smaller, targeted agricultural areas.

• Multispectral cameras: These are very near to satellite sensors, with additional benefits on spatial resolution. Therefore, details in information that give crop health assessment and pest detection can be availed through these cameras [6].
• Thermal cameras measure the thermal radiation that all surfaces emit, which very importantly serves the purposes of monitoring plant stress, irrigation management, and assessment of soil moisture.

Unmanned Aerial Vehicles (UAVs)

UAVs, otherwise called drones, have been used as versatile tools in precision agriculture since they can fly at lower altitudes and capture large extents of high-resolution imagery flexibly and cost-effectively [7].

Advantages: UAV real-time data acquisition sets the stage for crop growth stage monitoring, disease outbreak detection, and field variability assessments at high spatial resolutions with very high operational flexibility.

Data Acquisition and Preprocessing

Data Acquisition

Data acquisition activities must be carefully planned with detailed calibration for the respective sensors and image capture that can assure the quality and relevance of the collected data for subsequent agricultural applications. The main steps that are involved in data acquisition activities are:

• Plan: Determine the right time and frequency of data collection related to stages of crop growth and environmental factors.
• Calibration: Ensure sensor accuracy due to both radiometric and geometric calibration processes.
• Image Capture: Capture the images at certain times to avoid the interference of the atmosphere in order to have the maximum utility of the data.

Data Preprocessing

Raw data should be subjected to proper data pre-processing to correct all distortions, especially those related to sensors, and make it ready for proper analysis. The main steps that are involved in data pre-processing are:

• Radiometric correction: Adjust for the interferences from the atmosphere and the noise introduced by the sensors so that the sensor data output provides accurate reflectance values.
• Geometric correction: Coordinates the standard plane along which images are laid out, and thus, actually corrects for all those distortions introduced by the position of a sensor and the curvature of the Earth.
• Image enhancement: This stage improves the quality of images through contrast adjustment and filtering, aiming at helping one identify features of interest.

Data fusion literally means the integration of information from multiple sensors or systems to develop spatial and spectral resolution for enhancing interpretability in agricultural data processing.

GIS Uses in Agriculture

In recent times, the use of Geographic Information Systems has become part and parcel of agricultural practices since incorporating spatial data in every process of agriculture is very efficient in mapping and analysis and consequently, in making decisions. Formally, this section provides an outline of the roles of GIS in agriculture mapping and analysis, relevant GIS data layers, and general tools or software that are in use.

GIS in Agricultural Mapping and Analysis

GIS integrates spatial and non-spatial data so that farmers, agronomists, and researchers can visualize, analyze, and interpret agricultural information in a spatial format. Some of the most prominent roles of GIS in agriculture include: **Spatial Analysis:** GIS enables one to analyze spatial patterns, like soil variability, crop distribution, or terrain characteristics, which are significant in optimizing agricultural practice [8].

Precision Farming: GIS helps in precision farming by optimizing input usage according to spatial variability and enhancing crop yield and resource efficiency [9].

Decision Support Systems: Crop planning, disease monitoring, irrigation management, and yield prediction are some of the GIS-based systems employed in agriculture that use spatial data layers in conjunction with models and algorithms for their efficient working [10].

GIS Data Layers of Relevance to Agriculture

GIS relies on a diversity of spatial data layers that are essential for agricultural applications.

Topography and Elevation: Digital Elevation Models (DEMs) allow one to gain information on slope, aspect, and elevation, affecting water flow and, thus, soil erosion management [11].

Soil Type and Properties: Soil mapping helps to identify the type of soil with fertility and nutrient content, which is essential in planning effective soil management strategies and fertilizer application.

Land Use and Land Cover: The land-use/land-cover classification helps monitor changes in agricultural practices, urban expansion concerns, and ecosystem services [12].

Weather and Climate Data: Climate information, such as rainfall patterns, temperature variations, and frost occurrences, feeds into crop modeling and seasonal forecasting.

GIS Tools and Software

In agriculture, various GIS tools and software are employed to manage, analyze, and visualize spatial data, such as:

ArcGIS: Developed by Esri, ArcGIS is significant for managing spatial data, analysis, and visualization in farming.

QGIS: It is a free and open-source GIS software with similar functionality as ArcGIS. It is more budget-friendly for those in the agriculture sector.

GRASS GIS: Another open-source platform providing advanced spatial analysis and modeling capabilities tailored for agricultural applications.

Large Language Models (LLMs) and their Applications

LLMs are the most advanced artificial intelligence systems today. They use deep learning to understand and generate human-like text. Prominent examples include OpenAI's GPT-3 and GPT-4. Personally, GPT-3 has been trained on diverse internet text and has a capacity of 175 billion parameters. Thus, it is tailored to handle many hitherto language tasks, such as translation, summarization, and question-answering [13].

GPT-4 has improved accuracy, contextual sense, and efficient operations over GPT-3. Handling complex instructions with nuanced interpretation has made this generation better than the previous one and has made it more viable for specialized applications, such as in agriculture, fertilization, and pest management, to ensure effectiveness regarding productivity and sustainability of the crops. As shown in Fig. (**1**) , within LLMs, Multi-Layer Perceptrons (MLPs) play a crucial role.

Fine-Tuning of Pre-Trained LLM for Specific Applications

There are two steps to training an LLM: pre-training and fine-tuning. Pre-training exposes the model to significant texts where it finds general language patterns. Fine-tuning then takes these already pre-trained models and tunes them into specific applications by further training on domain-specific datasets.

For agricultural applications, fine-tuning involves training the model on datasets comprising agricultural research papers, sensor data annotations, and GIS reports. This specialized training enables LLMs to offer more pertinent and precise interpretations of agricultural data, including assessments of crop health, soil quality, and weather impact. Table **1** explains the training processes involved in LLMs [14].

The accuracy of the model in performing such tasks could be quantitatively calculated using the mean squared error as:

$$MSE = \frac{\Sigma(y_i - y'_i)^2}{N} \tag{1}$$

y_i, represents the true values, y'_i represents the predicted values, and N represents number of observations.

Table 1. Training process of LLMs.

Step	Description
Data Collection	Gathering vast amounts of textual data from various sources like books, websites, and articles.
Data Preprocessing	Cleaning and formatting the data, including tokenization, normalization, and handling missing data.
Model Architecture	Designing the neural network architecture, such as transformers, to process and learn from the data.
Training	Feeding the preprocessed data into the model to adjust the parameters using techniques like backpropagation.
Evaluation	Assessing the model's performance on validation datasets to fine-tune and improve accuracy.
Fine-Tuning	Further training the model on specific tasks or domains to enhance its capabilities.
Deployment	Implementing the trained model in real-world applications for tasks like text generation, translation, or summarization.
Monitoring and Maintenance	Continuously monitoring the model's performance and updating it as needed to ensure relevance and accuracy.

LLM Capabilities and Limitations in Analyzing Information

Capabilities of LLMs

The following are the capabilities of LLMs:

Natural Language Understanding: LLMs can understand and derive independent patterns from vast amounts of textual data.

Pattern Recognition: They are skilled in finding correlations and patterns of complex data sets, which could not have been found using any other technique of conventional analysis [15].

Prediction Modeling: LLMs help in making predictions based on past trends and enable decision-making. For example, predictive modeling may be based on a linear relationship, which is expressed mathematically as:

$$\hat{y} = W \cdot X + b \tag{2}$$

Where, $\hat{y}$ is the predicted outcome, W represents the weight matrix, X is the input feature vector, and b is the bias term.

Data Interpretation: It improves the values of remote sensing and GIS information by providing analytical context and recommendations.

Limitations of LLMs

The following are the limitations of LLMs:

Data Dependence: Diverse and good training data influence the quality of the output of LLMs, which can lead to inherent biases in their responses.

Computational Resources: Both the training and even fine-tuning of LLMs remain computationally expensive, demanding high computational resources.

Interpretability: LLMs cannot be very transparent in their decision-making processes, such that it might be quite difficult to understand how some specific conclusions have been achieved.

Contextual Errors: LLMs, being powerful, can, at times, commit errors based on ambiguous or out-of-context information.

Integrating LLMs with Remote Sensing and GIS

Coupling large language models with remote sensing and geographic information systems presents an integrated powerful way of improving analysis and decision-making in agricultural data. In this section, several techniques for fusing these technologies, their benefits, and practical agriculture applications are examined conclusively [16].

Data Fusion Technique

Data fusion refers to a process by which data from different sources can be combined in order to extract information that is more compatible, accurate, and informative than that available from any one source. Fusing such LLMs with RS and GIS calls for much sophistication since a wide variety in the types of data has to be equally fused.

Multi-Source Data Integration

It is the process of combining data from different and diverse sources into a unified, coherent dataset.

Remote Sensing Data: This should include satellite images, aerial photos, and UAV data.

GIS Data: This includes spatial layers concerning landscape information, such as soil maps, topography, land use, and crop types.

LLM Data: It consists of contextual data derived from research articles, sensor metadata, and field reports, as shown in Fig. (**2**) .

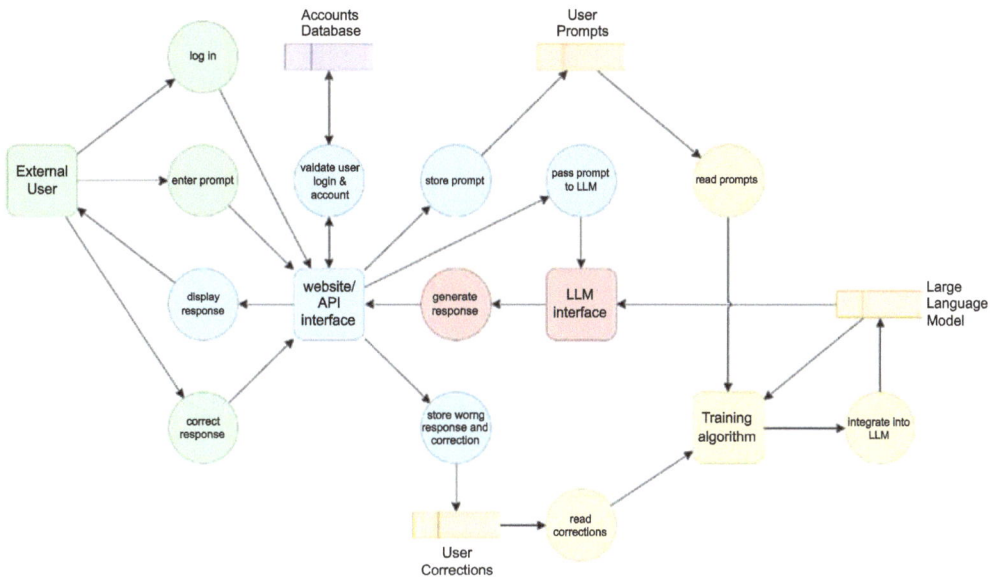

Fig. (2). Enhanced data interpretation with LLMs.

A data fusion model can be used to combine multiple sources of information into a unified dataset effectively, as:

$$D_{\text{fused}} = \alpha D1 + \beta D2 + \gamma D3 + \dots \tag{3}$$

Here, α, β, and γ are the weights assigned to each data source (D1, D2, D3, *etc.*), representing the relative importance of each data type.

NLP-Based Data Interpretation Model

Once the data is fused, it can provide insight by processing the textual data through an NLP model, as:

$$\text{Insight}_{LLM} = \sum_{i=1}^{N} \propto_i . \text{NLP}(Text_i) \tag{4}$$

Where, Insight$_{LLM}$ represents the overall insight extracted by the LLM.

α_i (alpha_i) represents the attention weight for the i-th piece of text (Text_i). These weights are calculated dynamically based on the importance of each text to the overall insight. NLP(Text_i) represents the output of an NLP (Natural Language Processing) function applied to the i-th piece of text (Text_i).

Contextual Analysis: Large language model integration allows the fusion of contextual understanding derived from textual data with spatial and temporal information, further enhancing the ability of LLMs to comprehend complex agricultural phenomena like weather effects on crop health.

Case Studies and Applications

Yield Prediction

A study conducted in the Midwest USA integrated satellite image data, soil maps, and historical yield data in predicting corn yield [17]. Field reports were presented and analyzed with an increased accuracy of 15% over traditional methods using LLMs by the researchers.

Pest and Disease Detection

In a recent study [18], the applicability of LLMs with UAV imagery and GIS data was assessed for the location and management of soybean crop pests in Brazil. Indeed, the literature and field reports provided by local land managers were analyzed, revealing that pests caused a percentage reduction in crop yield.

Case Study 1

Crop Monitoring and Yield Prediction

Using the developed integrated model for satellite images, soil maps, and historical yield data in the Midwestern United States, LLMs were used to predict corn yield. It is possible to improve model accuracy to reach 15% higher than that of the conventional method by fine-tuning using research articles and fieldmark reports [19].

Methodology

Satellite imagery was used to calculate the Normalized Difference Vegetation Index (NDVI), complemented by soil maps to enhance spatial analysis. Historical yield data were used for yield estimation.

A data fusion approach was employed to align spatial and temporal datasets at a feature level. LLMs were fine-tuned using agricultural research publications and field reports to improve contextual understanding. Finally, insights extracted from the LLMs were integrated into the predictive model for further refinement and accuracy enhancement.

Results and Discussions

This integrated approach did better in yield prediction since important information on the factors driving crop productivity was elicited. LLMs incorporated the most recent research findings, increasing adaptability under the changing conditions of this model.

Case Study 2

Pests and Disease Monitoring

In the region of Brazilian agribusiness, a study was conducted by integrating UAV imagery and GIS data, with LLMs for assessing pest outbreaks in soybean plants. The LLM developed a model based on scientific literature and field reports to evaluate the priorities it identified for reducing pest-related losses in this crop by 20%.

Methodology

Data sources: UAV images were used in monitoring the health of crops, along with GIS data for spatial analysis. Data fusion: Image data and spatial data were integrated at a feature level. LLM training: An LLM was trained using literature and field reports about pest management. Decision support: Informed recommendations were derived through the fusion of data and LLM insights. Results and discussion: Early detection of pest outbreaks was carried out with actionable recommendations on its management. Consequently, the deployment of LLMs resulted in enhancing the integration of the latest research and local field data to realize more effective pest control.

Applications in Agriculture

In the last two decades, there has been tremendous growth in agricultural practices concerning monitoring, analysis, and optimization of various farming activities through remote sensing, GIS, and LLMs. This chapter encapsulates several such applications concerning crop monitoring and yield prediction, soil health and nutrient management, pest and disease detection, and precision agriculture with decision support systems.

Crop Monitoring and Yield Prediction

Effective crop monitoring, with accurate yield prediction, ensures food security and BITTA agricultural productivity. While remote sensing and GIS offer valuable spatial and temporal data, LLMs improve the chances of correctly interpreting the data and enhancing predictive modeling.

Remote Sensing for Crop Monitoring

Satellite and UAV imagery provide insights into crop development stages, vegetation indices, such as NDVI, and biomass estimation. This information allows for the assessment of crop health, the recognition of stress factors, and the estimation of yields.

Yield Prediction Models

Yield prediction models are key tools in agriculture, integrating remote sensing data with historical yield records and other environmental variables for crop yield estimation. The integration of these various datasets enables the generation of predictions that help in planning and decision-making. An LLM fine-tuned on a corpus of agricultural literature and field reports can make complex patterns in the data, follow likely trends, and, importantly, tap expert knowledge to inform the predictions.

NDVI Calculation

One of the important components of yield prediction is that it can be scored based on vegetation health, customarily measured by the use of the Normalized Vegetation Difference Index (NDVI). The following formula is used to score NDVI:

$$NDVI = (NIR - R) / (NIR + R) \qquad (5)$$

NDVI, Normalized Difference Vegetation Index, is a value ranging between -1 to 1 that indicates the health and density of vegetation. NIR refers to the reflectance in the near-infrared band of the electromagnetic spectrum. Healthy vegetation reflects more near-infrared light than visible light.

R represents the reflectance in the red band of the electromagnetic spectrum. By integrating satellite and UAV image data into the GIS environment, monitoring and management strategies for agricultural fields have been more firmly established. Approaches illustrated in Fig. (**3**) demonstrate the use of NDVI for crop health monitoring, while Fig. (**4**) highlights the application of Synthetic Aperture Radar (SAR) for soil moisture estimation. Healthy vegetation absorbs more red light for photosynthesis, which contributes to the effectiveness of these remote sensing techniques.

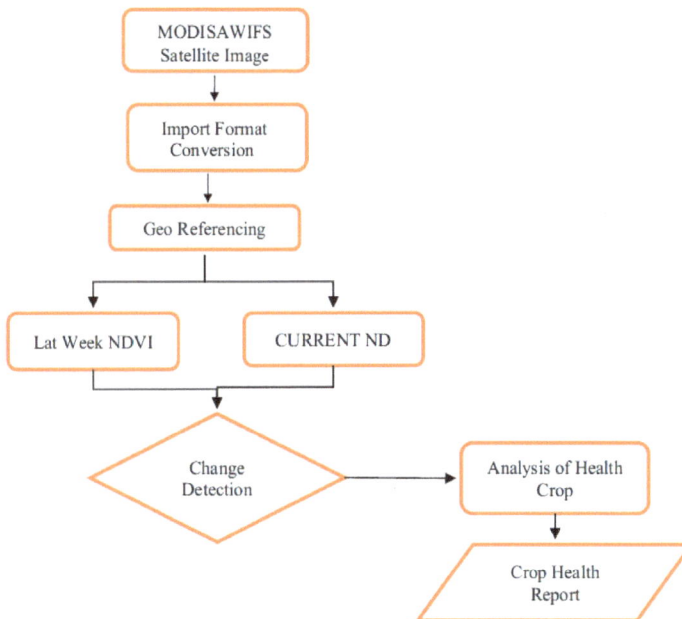

Fig. (3). NDVI-based crop health monitoring.

Soil Health and Nutrient Management

Soil health is fundamental to sustainable agriculture. Remote sensing and GIS generate detailed soil maps, while LLMs aid in the interpretation of complex soil data and nutrient management practices [20].

Remote sensing technologies, such as hyperspectral imaging and Synthetic Aperture Radar (SAR), provide data on soil properties, including moisture, organic matter content, and texture.

Nutrient Management

GIS integrates soil data with crop requirements, facilitating precise fertilizer application by ensuring that nutrients are applied in the right amount and at the right location. Adopting such precision agriculture methods is very important in optimizing crop yield at the same time as reducing environmental impact.

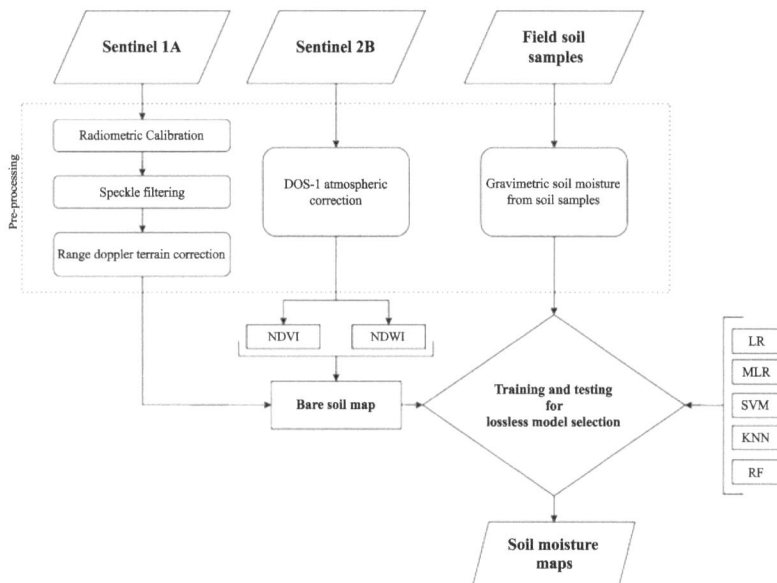

Fig. (4). Soil moisture map from SAR data.

LLMs go a step further to make this process more efficient by interpreting a large number of research articles and field data to provide location-specific suggestions on nutrient management, an example of which can be seen in Mulla 2013. One of the areas in precision agriculture is the control of the moisture content of the soil. It can be estimated by Synthetic Aperture Radar data. The local relationship between SAR backscatter and soil moisture content can be expressed as:

$$SM = a \cdot \sigma^0 + b \tag{6}$$

Where, SM is soil moisture content (dependent variable), a is a slope of the linear relationship (coefficient), $\sigma 0$ is Sigma term (independent variable), and b is the Y-intercept of the linear relationship.

Pest and Disease Detection

Early detection and management of pests and diseases are crucial for minimizing crop losses. The combination of remote sensing, GIS, and LLMs enhances the ability to detect and respond to pest and disease outbreaks.

Remote Sensing for Pest and Disease Detection

Multispectral and thermal imaging help identify stress patterns in crops that may indicate pest or disease presence.

LLMs in Pest Management

LLMs are instrumental in processing vast amounts of scientific literature and field reports to identify effective pest management strategies. By analyzing environmental conditions and historical data, these models can predict potential pest outbreaks, helping farmers take preventive measures and reduce crop damage. One of the key measures of pest and disease management is the incidence rate, IR. It quantifies the proportion affected by a certain disease in a population. Its formula is as follows:

$$IR = (N\_d / N\_t) \times 100 \qquad (7)$$

Where, IR is infection rate, a percentage value indicating the proportion of a population infected. N_d is the Number of individuals infected with a disease. N_t is the total number of individuals in the population.

Enterprise-wide AI: Precisive Agriculture and Decision Support Systems

Precision farming is oriented towards optimum resource use and productivity enhancement by precision monitoring and management practices. Remote sensing, GIS, and LLM together associate with decision support systems that offer actionable insights for the same.

Precision Agriculture Techniques

The technologies, including VRT and automated machinery, use spatial data to provide for optimum planting, fertilization, and harvesting.

Decision Support Systems

DSS relies on spatial data layers, predictive models, and LLM-generated insights for farmers to make effective decisions in crop management, irrigation, and pest control. The workflow of the Decision Support System for precision agriculture is shown in Fig. (**5**) .

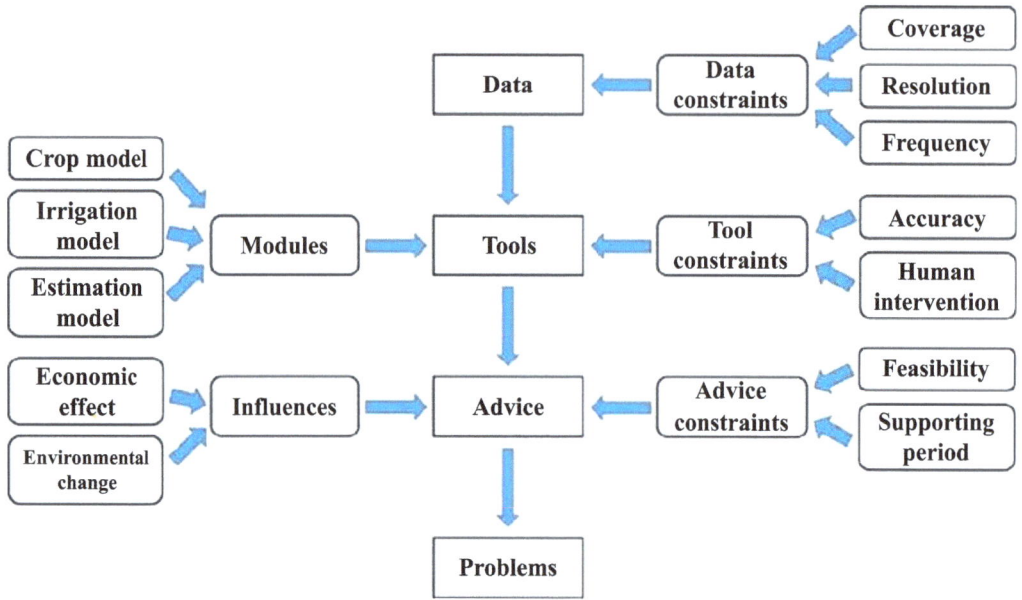

Fig. (5). Decision support system workflow for precision agriculture.

The precision fertilization rate can be calculated as:

$$FR = (Yt - Yc) / RUE \qquad (8)$$

Where, FR is a fraction of radiation used in photosynthesis (dependent variable), and its value ranges between 0 and 1. Yt is the total incoming photosynthetically active radiation (PAR) intercepted by the plant canopy (independent variable). Yc is photosynthetically active radiation (PAR) not absorbed by the plant canopy (independent variable). This radiation is either reflected or transmitted.

RUE is the Radiation Use Efficiency (constant). This is a specific value for a particular plant or plant type and represents the amount of biomass produced per unit of PAR absorbed.

CONCLUSION

This chapter discusses the main findings of the various prior studies, reflects on their implications for future research and practice, and sums up its final reflections on integrating remote sensing, GIS, and Large Language Models in agriculture. Moreover, it explains how remote sensing, GIS, and LLMs may be integrated for a radical total transformation of agriculture.

By integrating satellite and UAV image data into the GIS environment, monitoring and management strategies for agricultural fields have been more firmly established. Advanced approaches to data fusion can be applied in reconciling heterogeneous data sources, thus enabling high accuracy and consistency of all agricultural data. LLMs serve as a central component in providing analytical data, contextual understanding, and insights, capabilities that traditional methods often lack. This integration of remote-sensing technology with GIS and LLMs within agricultural operations opens up new prospects for research in the future and practical applications in real life. Better models and algorithms need to be developed that can handle and analyze larger data sets with a greater degree of accuracy. In the future, to make the models more robust and reliable, further research is required.

There is a necessity for scalable solutions that can be more easily and quickly rolled out for use amongst farmers and agricultural practitioners. This involves, across the world, user-friendly interfaces and technologies that are affordable to farmers. This requires collaboration among agronomists, data scientists, remote sensing experts, and policymakers for such complex challenges in agriculture to provide holistic and innovative solutions through interdisciplinary research. This would be the critical goal for future research in light of sustainable agricultural practices and resilience to climate change. Management plans that integrate models of agriculture with environmental data help mitigate plans that will lessen the impacts of climate change on agriculture.

REFERENCES

[1]   Xue J, Su B. Significant remote sensing vegetation indices: A review of developments and applications. J Sens 2017; 2017(1): 1-17.
[http://dx.doi.org/10.1155/2017/1353691]

[2]   Gebbers R, Adamchuk VI. Precision agriculture and food security. Science 2010; 327(5967): 828-31.
[http://dx.doi.org/10.1126/science.1183899] [PMID: 20150492]

[3]   Zhang X, Friedl MA, Schaaf CB, Strahler AH, Schneider A. The footprint of urbanclimates on vegetationphenology. Geophys Res Lett 2004; 31(12).

[4]   Brown TB. Languagemodels are few-shot learners. arXivpreprint. arXiv:200514165 2020.

[5]   Toth C, Jóźków G. Remote sensing platforms and sensors: A survey. ISPRS J Photogramm Remote Sens 2016; 115: 22-36.
[http://dx.doi.org/10.1016/j.isprsjprs.2015.10.004]

[6]   Sishodia RP, Ray RL, Singh SK. Applications of remote sensing in precision agriculture: A review. Remote Sens (Basel) 2020; 12(19): 3136.
[http://dx.doi.org/10.3390/rs12193136]

[7]   Thenkabail PS, Aneece I, Teluguntla P, *et al.* Hyperspectral remote sensing for terrestrial applications. InRemote Sensing Handbook 2016; III: 285-358. [CRC Press.].

[8]   Li J, Heap AD. A review of spatial interpolation methods for environmental scientists. Performance and impact factors, Ecological Informatics, 6, 3–4, 2011, 228-241, 1574-9541. [http://dx.doi.org/10.1016/j.ecoinf.2010.12.003]

[9]   Yousefi MR, Razdari AM. Application of GIS and GPS in precision agriculture (a review). Int J Adv Biol Biomed Res 2015; 3(1): 7-9.

[10]   Kadiyala MDM, Nedumaran S, Singh P, S C, Irshad MA, Bantilan MCS. An integrated crop model and GIS decision support system for assisting agronomic decision making under climate change. Sci Total Environ 2015; 521-522: 123-34. [http://dx.doi.org/10.1016/j.scitotenv.2015.03.097] [PMID: 25829290]

[11]   Thomas IA, Jordan P, Shine O, *et al.* Defining optimal DEM resolutions and point densities for modelling hydrologically sensitive areas in agricultural catchments dominated by microtopography. Int J Appl Earth Obs Geoinf 2017; 54: 38-52. [http://dx.doi.org/10.1016/j.jag.2016.08.012]

[12]   Foley JA, DeFries R, Asner GP, *et al.* Global consequences of land use. Science 2005; 309(5734): 570-4.

[13]   Brown TB. Language models are few-shot learners. arXiv preprint arXiv:200514165 2020.

[14]   Silva B, Nunes L, Estevão R, Aski V, Chandra R. GPT-4 as an agronomist assistant? Answering agriculture exams using large language models. arXiv preprint arXiv:231006225 2023.

[15]   Awais M, Alharthi AH, Kumar A, Cholakkal H, Anwer RM. AgroGPT: Efficient agricultural vision-language model with expert tuning. arXiv preprint arXiv:241008405 2024.

[16]   Wang J, Wang Y, Li G, Qi Z. Integration of remote sensing and machine learning for precision agriculture: a comprehensive perspective on applications. Agronomy (Basel) 2024; 14(9): 1975. [http://dx.doi.org/10.3390/agronomy14091975]

[17]   Sapkota R, Qureshi R, Hassan SZ, *et al.* Multi-modal LLMs in agriculture: A comprehensive review. Authorea Preprints 2024. [http://dx.doi.org/10.36227/techrxiv.172651082.24507804/v1]

[18]   Raman RK, Kumar A, Sarkar S, *et al.* Reconnoitering precision agriculture and resource management: A comprehensive review from an extension standpoint on artificial intelligence and machine learning. Indian Res J Ext Educ 2024; 24(1): 108-23.

[19]   Wu B, Zhang M, Zeng H, *et al.* Challenges and opportunities in remote sensing-based crop monitoring: a review. Natl Sci Rev 2023; 10(4): nwac290. [http://dx.doi.org/10.1093/nsr/nwac290] [PMID: 36960224]

[20]   Nawar S, Corstanje R, Halcro G, Mulla D, Mouazen AM. Delineation of soil management zones for variable-rate fertilization: A review. Adv Agron 2017; 143: 175-245. [http://dx.doi.org/10.1016/bs.agron.2017.01.003]

CHAPTER 4

Technological Integration and Economic Sustainability in Agriculture: A Systematic Literature Review

Napoleon Prabakaran[1,*], Navaneethakumar Venugopal[1] and Vijaya Gangoor[1]

[1] CMS Business School, JAIN (Deemed-to-be University), Bengaluru, Karnataka, India

Abstract: This article presents a comprehensive literature analysis that examines the relationship between technology adoption and integration with economics in the agricultural sector, with the aim of promoting sustainability. This study employed a comprehensive literature analysis to examine the existing body of research on agriculture within the field of business and management. The analysis focused on how management journals address agricultural topics (Agri-business). Established best practices for literature review were used to ensure a robust and systematic approach. The analysis identified eight overarching themes in the field of agriculture in business and management: Adoption and diffusion of technologies, blockchain technology and transparency, precision farming and sustainability, farmer information needs and adoption, Community Supported Agriculture (CSA) and digital platforms, participatory action research and agroecosystem restoration, innovation networks and sustainability, and circular economy in agriculture. The article emphasizes areas where study is lacking and provides potential avenues for future research based on these crucial topics.

Keywords: Agriculture, Economics, Sustainability, Systematic literature review, Technology.

INTRODUCTION

Being the backbone of the global economy, agriculture is faced with increasing difficulties as the population of the planet keeps rising [1]. With the estimated 9.7 billion worldwide population in 2025, food demand is expected to climb significantly. Climate change is also negatively affecting agriculture concurrently; these consequences are projected to become more severe in the future [2, 3]. Furthermore, resources such as water, land, and other basic necessities are becoming increasingly restricted [4, 5].

* **Corresponding author Napoleon Prabakaran:** CMS Business School, JAIN (Deemed-to-be University), Bengaluru, Karnataka, India; E-mail: nepoleonbonoparte@gmail.com

Raghavendra M. Devadas, Vani Hiremani, Praveen Gujjar Jagannath, Lubna Ambreen & Harold Andrew Patrick (Eds.)

Among these urgent problems, agriculture struggles with a paradox: poor acceptance of novel technology [6, 7]. Precision agriculture and other technical developments have great promise, although their rate of application is shockingly low. This is a lost chance to use drought-resistant crops during times of water shortage or to reach the intended 70% increase in food output by 2025 or otherwise [8]. Beyond the understanding level of individual farmers, the obstacles to technology adoption are several and go beyond their own perspective. Limited internet access, language obstacles, and resistance to accepting new technology are just a few of the difficulties small-scale farmers in underdeveloped areas can face [9, 10]. Further aggravating these problems are systematic ones including limited loan availability and poor infrastructure [11, 12]. The complicated interaction between human limitations and more general challenges makes it difficult to apply creative agricultural ideas meant to revolutionize the sector and guarantee food security.

Dealing with the causes of farmers' resistance to adopting agricultural innovations is not only a scholarly activity but also an essential one [13]. Technology has great promise given the approaching issue of global food insecurity, the effect of climate change on crops, and the limited resource availability [14]. Unlocking the promise of these breakthroughs depends on overcoming the difficult obstacles of personal limitations and institutionalized impediments [15]. By means of this methodical evaluation of the literature, we hope to be able to empower farmers, guide policies, and close the digital gap, thereby enabling a more sustainable and fair future for everyone [15, 16].

METHOD

A systematic review is a thorough and deliberate way to synthesize available research on a certain issue [17 - 19]. It entails spotting, assessing, and combining all pertinent studies to offer a whole picture of the present level of knowledge and point up areas for future study. By means of summary, integration, and synthesis of the corpus of current literature, systematic reviews assist in understanding what has been done, what has been learned, and what remains to be investigated [20].

Usually, the approach to performing a systematic review is strict. It starts with specifying the study question and choosing pertinent keywords to direct the search of the literature. Then methodically investigated academic databases and other sources are published works relevant to the study subject uncovered. The most relevant studies for the review are chosen using predefined inclusion and exclusion criteria. Before the data is gathered and aggregated from these particular investigations, its quality and validity are carefully evaluated. At last, the results are examined and explained to spot trends, patterns, and gaps in the body of current research [20, 21].

Designed to be open, repeatable, and reduce prejudice, the methodical review process follows a specified and orderly procedure [22]. Its thorough character enables scholars to have a full awareness of the present level of knowledge on a given issue and guides further lines of inquiry.

Step 1: Data Search and Collection Process

We used the four main procedures described in a study [23] for systematic literature review: Choosing the correct database; spotting pertinent keywords; building a thorough search string; and then retrieving the pertinent data. We used Elsevier's Scopus, a reliable and extensively used tool with indexing of a large number of peer-reviewed publications, for the database [24]. Scopus is one useful and well-known tool for undertaking systematic literature reviews as it includes around 97% of the articles listed in the Web of Science (WoS) database [23]. Furthermore, a number of researchers have suggested and used Scopus extensively for systematic reviews [25 - 27], further enhancing its standing as a thorough and trustworthy source for scholarly literature.

This study included a number of point of views from disciplines like sustainability, economics, technology, and agriculture. We aimed to find terms covering the aspect of economy, technology, and agriculture. We adopted the approaches and vocabulary used in a study referenced as [22, 25], which investigated the management issues of agriculture, particularly with an eye toward the intersections of agriculture and economics, agriculture and technology, and agriculture and sustainability, respectively. Our search included agricultural-related phrases together with technology, economics, sustainability, and sustainability as shown in Fig. (**1**). We followed standard guidelines [26, 27] to include papers that could have used varied wording. We then gathered information and converted the main terms into search strings. Using an asterisk (*) as a wildcard—which may represent any single character, absent character, or numerous characters in a phrase—we performed the search. For instance, the searched word "agri*" might yield results on agriculture, agritech, agribusiness, and so on. The study was conducted particularly on the Scopus title-abstract-keyword page. April of 2024 was the month when we received the information. Following more rigorous methodological rules later, the data collected was limited to peer-reviewed publications, omitting conference papers, book chapters, and book chapters. The search resulted in 1124 publications.

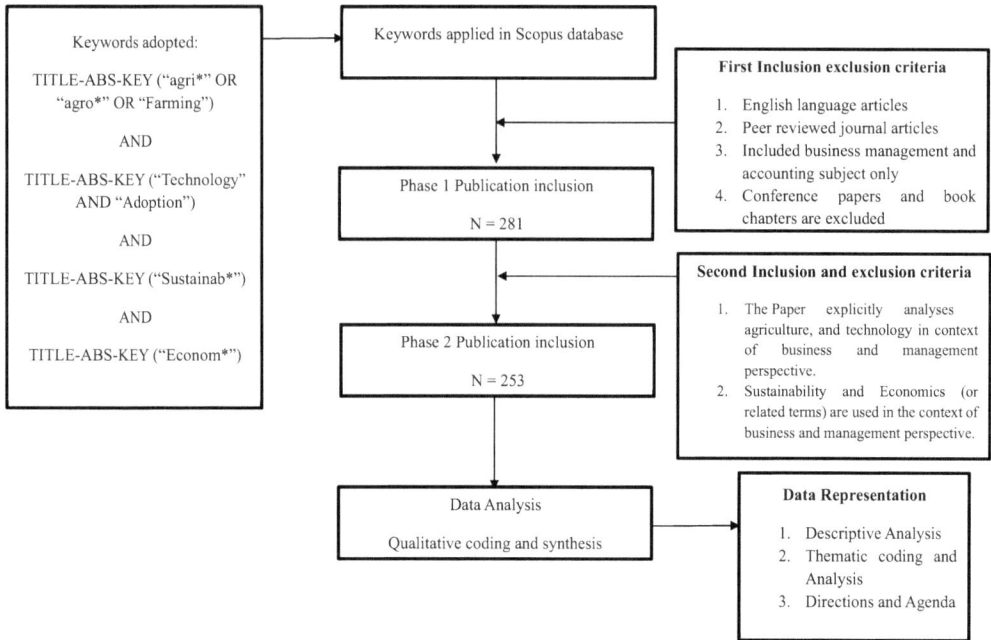

Fig. (1). Data delimitation process.

Step 2: Inclusion/exclusion Criteria

There are 372 papers on the topic of business management and accounting in the Scopus database overall. We have decided to just accept papers falling under the area of business and management as our review is from the point of view of corporate management in agriculture. A total of 281 articles were collected, and we devised inclusion criteria in order to pick the pertinent publications from among them [27]. This was done in order to guarantee that the selection of the literature would be objective and comprehensive. By careful title and abstract analysis, the writers verified the conformance of the 253 papers with the inclusion criteria. The admittance requirements followed this: The study has to specifically examine technology in the framework of agriculture and use economics and sustainability—or comparable language—in the same regard. After several meetings, the writers agreed on the inclusion and exclusion rules. Following this procedure, 253 papers in all were gathered for the last review. All the authors went over the 253 papers once again to guarantee their legitimacy and clear any questions.

Step 3: Review the Method Adopted to Examine the Data

Several approaches allow one to evaluate systematic reviews [17, 27]. In our work [28], we developed a special data structure using an inductive method. Other recent systematic literature reviews in allied domains have also made use of this method [19]. The study applied a qualitative coding system [23, 30] (Table **1**). Before starting the study of the individual papers, we noted the traits of the pool of acquired materials on economics, technology, and agriculture in business and management.

Table 1. Shows the codes to obtain the final themes of the study.

First Order Codes	Second Order Themes	Aggregate Theme
1. Contextual factors like education, land size, and access to knowledge. 2. Situations of each farmer 3. Knowledge sharing through social media channels.	**Facilitating technology adoption**	*Adoption and diffusion of technologies*
1. Recommendation by peers. 2. Subsidies, training, and regulations.	**Influencing technology adoption**	
1. Enhanced Traceability. 2. Improved accountability. 3. Reducing counterfeit products.	**Benefits of blockchain**	*Blockchain Technology and Transparency*
1. Infrastructure limitations. 2. Cost barriers. 3. Lack of standardization.	**Challenges in blockchain**	
1. Resource utilization. 2. Data-driven insights. 3. Improved efficiency. 4. Positive outcomes.	**Outcomes of precision farming**	*Precision Farming and Sustainability*
1. Collaboration networks. 2. Government incentives. 3. Peer-to-peer learning.	**Solutions for wider adoption**	
1. Traditional Channels. 2. Rise of Mobile Ag-Apps.	**Technologies for information**	*Farmer Information Needs and Adoption*
1. Location-Specific Information. 2. Credibility and Trust. 3. Information Quality Concerns.	**Information quality**	
1. User-Centric Design. 2. Real-Time Knowledge Access. 3. Culturally Sensitive Apps.	**Platform design**	
1. Cooperative Ownership. 2. Crowdfunding. 3. Engaged Consumers.	**Social and solidarity economy integration**	*Community Supported Agriculture (CSA) and Digital Platforms*
1. Online Platforms. 2. Data-Driven Practices. 3. Promoting Sustainability.	**Professionalized and tech-Savvy**	

(Table 1) cont.....

First Order Codes	Second Order Themes	Aggregate Theme
1. Importance of farmer participation. 2. Power of Participatory Action. 3. Collaboration for improved solutions.	**Collaborative actions**	*Participatory Action Research and Agroecosystem Restoration*
1. Co-monitoring for trust and sustainability. 2. Knowledge sharing and skill development.	**Implementation and empowerment**	
1. Customization over generic solutions. 2. Farmer-led restoration for long-term success.	**Restoration approach**	
1. Connecting farmers, researchers, NGOs, and corporations. 2. Accelerate innovation of sustainable practices.	**Innovative approaches**	*Innovation Networks and Sustainability*
1. Integration with existing structures. 2. bridge the gap between innovation and implementation. 3. facilitate peer-to-peer learning.	**Integrative implementation**	
1. Linear take-make-dispose model reaching its limit. 2. Food production by closing the resource loop and reducing waste.	**Limitation and opportunity**	*Circular Economy in Agriculture*
1. New technologies. 2. Easy to integrate. 3. Easy to see and understand.	**Incentivizing farmers**	
1. Education for knowledge and implementation. 2. Government policies and incentives.	**Education and policy support**	

First, we had to develop a coding and analysis system if we were to carefully review the papers. Three phases comprised the selected operation [28 - 30]. Using phrases taken from the papers, two authors carefully examined and classified every document at the first step. Commonly referred to as a first-order (informant-centered) analysis, this technique highlighted different features of every article, so we confirmed the coherence across authors, and entered this information into an Excel file [31, 32]. The study's initial codes reflected its various facets, such as its purpose, the technological, economical, and sustainable contexts under investigation, the level of inquiry (from individual farms to national levels), the variables that impact or predict sustainability, economics, technology, and agriculture from a managerial and business standpoint, and the results of these factors (Table **1**).

Phase two consisted of a second-order thematic analysis to position the data within constructs, variables, and contexts that are relevant to theory in the domains of agriculture, economics, technology, and sustainability in business and management. We thus moved to a higher degree of abstraction and suggested a way to combine first-order codes to create themes or clusters of articles with comparable theoretical connections or orientations. This method helped us to precisely identify the recurrent trends in the sample [30]. Following our agreement upon an appropriate set of first-order codes and utilizing those codes to create second-order themes, we further arranged our data in a hierarchical manner in the third step. The authors reached a consensus on how to include, integrate, and modify the overarching themes after conducting an analysis of the most important topics [29]. Currently, we have created a data structure that acts as a graphic representation of this data organizing mechanism. Under more general subjects like agriculture, economics, technology, and sustainability, the representation shows a hierarchical organization of second-order themes and their linked first-order labels inside the context of business and management [24].

THEMATIC EVALUATIONS OF PAST RESEARCH

Adoption and Diffusion of Technologies

Using sustainable agricultural technology requires consideration of several factors influencing farmers' acceptance of these technologies [33]. Farmers' degree of education, the size of their field, and their information access all affect their willingness to apply new technologies like precision farming [34]. Higher-educated people, those who own more property, and those who have internet access are more likely to accept these technologies. Conversely, farmers with restricted means might need tailored solutions [35].

Promoting the adoption of new methods and helping information to be transferred depends critically on social networks and extension services [36]. Farmers often learn from one another, building trust and reducing supposed risks connected to the adoption of new technology by means of mutual knowledge [36]. Providing training and bridging the gap between research and real application depend critically on extension programs [37]. Farmer field schools and other participatory approaches provide farmers with the tools to take charge of their own education and encourage group knowledge exchange [36].

Government policies and incentives have a major influence on the adoption rates [35]. Effective incentives for farmers to accept and apply sustainable technology are government ones including subsidies, tax breaks, and training programs [38]. Either too little infrastructure or too tight regulations could hinder development

[39]. Policies supporting research, networks of innovation, and stakeholder cooperation will help to reach long-term sustainability [40].

Using sustainable agricultural technology is a complex process affected by many social, financial, environmental, and institutional problems [40]. It is important to recognize the range of agricultural communities and modify methods [41]. By means of social networks, extension services, and participatory techniques, allowing the flow of knowledge might help build trust and lower apparent risks [41]. Moreover, government rules, incentives, and infrastructure supporting sustainable practices help speed up their implementation and growth [42].

Blockchain Technology and Transparency

By offering safe and open ledger systems, blockchain technology has become a possible substitute to change agricultural supply chains [43]. Farmers and consumers benefit from this technology as it allows every step of food production to be watched and recorded [44]. Blockchain technology presents farmers with a way to provide indisputable proof of their certifications and sustainable methods, therefore enabling more fair pricing [45]. Customers who want ethical manufacturing and openness might use blockchain issues in counterfeiting and item source misrepresentation [46].

Still, there are challenges like limits in infrastructure and high implementation costs [50]. Particularly smaller farms may find the costs to be unaffordable [46]. Furthermore, compatibility issues across several blockchain systems restrict the whole capacity of technology and are a hindrance to data exchange [45].

Stakeholders must cooperate if they want to solve these problems [46]. By putting policies that support blockchain use while protecting data privacy into effect, governments can help blockchain acceptance [47]. Resources must be distributed to build infrastructure and carry out initiatives to help smaller farms in adopting and efficiently using technology [48]. Implementing standardized and open-source technologies helps solve interoperability issues thereby guaranteeing easy data transfer [33].

Providing customers with knowledge about the benefits of sustainably produced items with traceability will help farmers be motivated to apply blockchain technologies [49]. Adopting a full approach that considers several elements like infrastructure, cost, compatibility, law, capacity building, and consumer awareness would help one to properly harness the potential of blockchain in agriculture [42]. Through cooperation, the agriculture industry can build confidence, guarantee accountability, and promote sustainable practices all across the supply chain [50].

Precision Farming and Sustainability

Using data-driven technology, precision farming helps maximize agricultural output while lessening negative environmental impact [49]. Therefore, essential information provided by soil sensors and drones enhances sustainability and profitability by means of their respective applications [50]. According to a study [51], farmers have the capacity to increase agricultural output by carefully managing resources such as water, seeds, and fertilizer. Examples of such resources include water. Still, there are challenges to the general acceptance and application of this technology, including ignorance and the initial outlay of costs [52]. Working together, networks linking farmers with experts might help solve these problems [53]. Certain routines or behaviors are further encouraged by government incentives such as tax cuts [53].

When a farmer obtains government assistance and learns from a wealthy neighbor, for example, they can decide to use precision irrigation techniques, thereby increasing water efficiency [54]. Participatory approaches and cooperative innovation enable farmers to empower themselves, hence increasing the effective adoption rate [55]. Considering factors such as farm size and resource availability, are context-specific precision farming solutions [55]. Tackling a wide spectrum of agricultural challenges depends on constant research and cooperation [56].

Farmer Information Needs and Adoption

In today's agricultural context, timely and relevant information is critical for making sound decisions [57]. With benefits including enabling contacts with others and real-time updates on weather and market prices, mobile social media apps have profoundly changed the way individuals receive and distribute knowledge [58]. These programs are particularly helpful in rural areas with limited traditional information sources [58].

However, farmers want information that is directly relevant to their unique requirements, and the quality and dependability of information offered by different programs might vary [59]. Platforms should offer accurate and region-specific information in a way that is simple for users to comprehend and utilize in order to build confidence [60]. Designing applications with farmers as the target audience is absolutely important as they have readily understandable material [55]. To enhance farm optimization and sustainability, these applications should offer farmers a seamless and uninterrupted process of acquiring information and implementing it in practice.

Innovation Networks and Sustainability

Innovative networks must promote collaboration in order for sustainable agriculture to succeed [61]. These networks, which include farmers, researchers, Non-Governmental Organizations (NGOs), and businesses, speed up the process of developing new ideas and stimulate the adoption of practices that are favourable to the environment [60]. Still, success depends on finding a fit with already-existing corporate networks [61].

Of great relevance is the careful integration of sustainable practices into current corporate networks [61]. Promoting sustainable practices by means of joint efforts with suppliers to offer environmentally friendly options at reasonable costs or by means of partnerships with retailers ready to pay a premium for sustainably grown products helps embrace sustainable practices [62].

The primary hubs for the knowledge-exchange and skill-building growth of innovation networks are: peer-to--peer learning, or the sharing of information between academics and farmers, which accelerates the application of innovative and creative ideas [63, 64]. Connecting sustainable approaches with their actual application, these networks foster collaboration and knowledge sharing.

Community Supported Agriculture (CSA) and Digital Platforms

Programs such as Community Supported Agencies (CSA) link customers straight to nearby farms, therefore fostering community, ethical consumption, and sustainable practices [65]. It can be difficult to ensure long-term viability and expand their scope [65]. Creative methods to improve the CSA model are based on digital technologies and Social Solidarity Economy (SSE) concepts [66]. Local CSAs can expand their reach and facilitate purchases by connecting consumers with online platforms [67]. Cooperative ownership and crowdsourcing are two examples of social and solidarity economy models that can let CSAs get over financial obstacles and guarantee sustainability [68]. For instance, a CSA that is administered as a cooperative by producers and consumers promotes adaptability and collective responsibility. Professionalized CSAs using ICTs and data are more likely to advocate sustainable behaviours [68]. While social media participation shows sustainability pledges, data analytics can help lower waste and raise crop yields [69]. Customers looking for moral food options are drawn to its openness and effectiveness. CSAs may increase community engagement, promote sustainable agriculture, and guarantee long-term survival by combining digital platforms and ideas of a social solidarity economy by means of these elements [61]. Shared ownership models and technology can help consumers and producers to be more transparent, reliable , and show their influence [62].

Participatory Action Research and Agroecosystem Restoration

Reviving and preserving our agroecosystems depend on farmers' active participation and collaboration rather than only technology developments. An efficient approach for doing this is participatory action research (PAR) [15]. Imagine an environment in which academics and farmers work together to develop cutting-edge technology and techniques for making decisions. This approach, which is implemented by farmers themselves, tailors solutions to their unique needs and circumstances, thereby increasing the probability of success and long-term sustainability [19].

Farmers might choose to collaborate with experts to test fresh approaches to soil preservation. Traditional knowledge would be exchanged in this cooperation together with practice adjustment to fit their particular surroundings [28]. This cooperative approach helps farmers, boosts confidence, and produces the acceptance and continuous use of these answers [37]. Important are knowledge distribution and skill development [39]. Participatory monitoring and assessment work beyond the simple data-collecting process. Imagine a cooperation between academics and farmers assessing new approaches to soil quality, agricultural output, and biodiversity [49]. With the knowledge and experience to make wise decisions, this cooperative approach helps farmers to accept responsibility for their land and analyzes the efficiency of solutions [51].

The availability of agricultural tools is not enough, they must be tailored to fit the particular needs of farmers [53]. Consider equipping farmers with sophisticated data analysis software to compensate for their inadequate computer skills. This alienation leads to discontent and stunts development. Individualized training, necessary resources, and user-friendly tools for agricultural practitioners are necessary [60]. Making data collection easier through the creation of mobile apps or providing area-specific training on sustainable practices are two possible ways to achieve this goal. The long-term viability of these initiatives is ensured by active participation in the restoration process. We may move away from a hierarchical approach and create a cooperative, information-sharing, and empowerment-promoting atmosphere by using the Participatory Action Research. Farmers play proactive leadership roles in the recovery of agroecosystems, therefore guaranteeing environmental well-being and food security for the next generations.

Circular Economy in Agriculture

Long-term maintenance of the present agricultural paradigm depends on resources and effective agriculture methods . By lowering waste and building a closed-loop system, the circular economy offers a pragmatic means of attaining sustainable food output [3]. Imagine an agricultural complex where wastewater is recycled for irrigation, wasted food is fed to cattle, and animal feces is transformed into fertilizers [28]. By using this cyclical approach, dependence on outside resources reduces, which lowers costs, and lessens the environmental impact [42].

It is crucial to consider factors such as the benefits of alternative approaches, how well they match their present ways, and how readily they can be seen and understood when trying to convince farmers to use circular approaches [42]. More attractive than traditional methods, farmers discover a fresh composting technology that generates better fertilizer at less cost [68]. When technology is seamlessly integrated with existing practices and offers clear benefits, it is more likely to be adopted [68]. In this sense, education serves a vital and indispensable role. Farmers who have a thorough awareness of composting, nitrogen cycling, and integrated farm management have the expertise to make well-informed decisions and use circular solutions customized to their particular needs and available resources [36].

Research on circular technologies may speed up through the use of government rules and incentives, which can also provide financial aid for implementation and provide the groundwork for a circular economy in agriculture [28]. Financial benefits for farms using government help for the purchase of composting equipment or circular processes [69]. This support might help to link the knowledge of a topic with its useful application. We can fully use the circular economy in agriculture by giving relative advantage, compatibility, visibility, and education top priority. For farmers, this method offers financial and environmental advantages as well as creates self-sustaining systems that advance the welfare of the land and its occupants.

CONCEPTUAL FRAMEWORK

A careful balance between maximizing profitability and production, reducing environmental harm, and supporting social justice is what defines sustainable agriculture [8, 26]. In order to facilitate a more sustainable future, digital technologies have the potential to profoundly alter agricultural practices. In this sense, they have become quite effective instruments [6]. But in order to fully realize this potential, one needs to have a thorough understanding of the intricate relationships between various technologies, implementation barriers [14, 37], stakeholder involvement [9, 68], and broader societal concerns [48, 71]. Using the given conceptual framework shown in Fig. (**2**), this study of the complex network investigates important problems and suggests directions for further investigation.

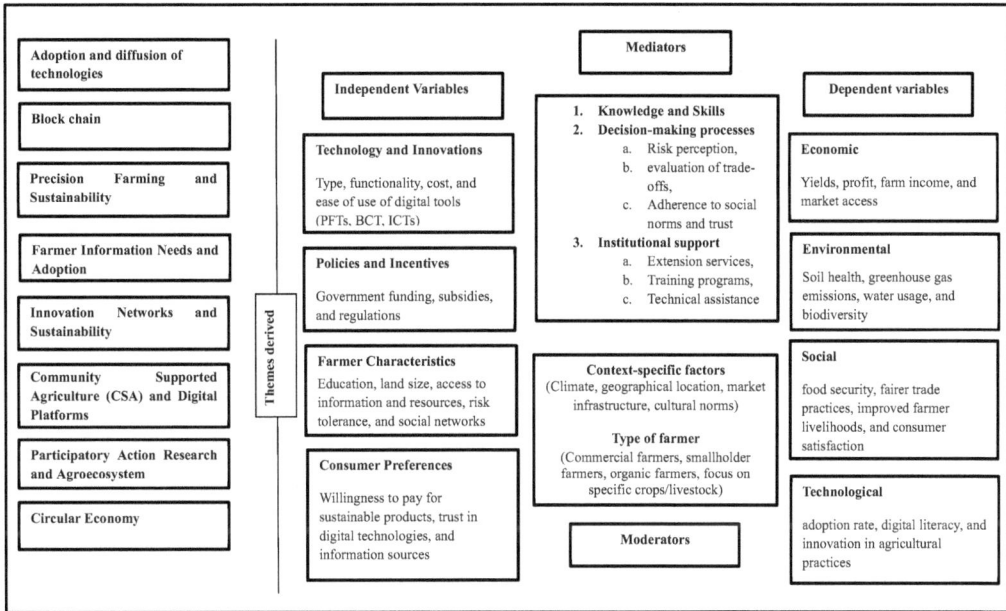

Fig. (2). Conceptual framework.

Outcomes

A number of elements including economic, environmental, social, and technical elements promote the quest for sustainability in the agriculture industry. From an economic standpoint, increased agricultural output, financial gain, farm revenue, and increased market entry become critical determinants that influence farmers' lives and strengthen the agricultural industry's long-term viability [25, 52]. Concurrent with this is environmental sustainability achieved by giving projects improving soil health top priority, reducing greenhouse gas emissions, careful water usage top importance, and protection of biodiversity top priority [5, 70]. The long-term sustainability of agricultural practices is ensured by this system, which also safeguards the environment. The benefits that sustainability brings to society are clear and include, but are not limited to, better food security, happier customers, and stronger farmer livelihoods [1, 7, 8]. The resilience and equality of society that are essential for the agriculture sector's sustained growth are fostered by these elements working together. Finally, as shown by the increased adoption of digital technologies, improved digital literacy, and creative agricultural methods that support both productivity and adaptability [10, 37], technological progress has a great influence. The interdependence among these economic, environmental, social, and technical elements emphasizes the all-encompassing character of sustainability in the agricultural sector and supports a harmonic cohabitation between human activities and the ecosystems depending on them.

Predictors

Many pushing forces affect the results of agricultural sustainability; among them, technology and innovations are quite important. Adoption and general efficacy of digital tools including Blockchain Technology (BCT) [14, 37], Information and Communication Technologies [11, 26, 61], and Precision Farming Technologies (PFTs) [15, 26, 50] have a great influence on their adoption. Moreover, the policies and incentives passed by authorities significantly affect the surroundings [39, 45]. Regulatory frameworks, government support, and subsidies [8, 33] greatly affect the degree to which technology is embraced and sustainable farming practices are included. Moreover, in this specific setting, the capacity and choices of individual producers are very important [31, 43]. Different farmer characteristics including the level of education, the extent of land holdings, availability of information and resources, risk tolerance, and social contacts together affect the rate at which sustainable practices are adopted and technology is included at the local level [9, 45, 48]. The numerous individual actions taken within the agriculture sector as a whole influence its general sustainability by means of their impact on other sectors. Furthermore, the interdependence of the web reaches customer preferences, which are rather important in determining the dynamics of the market [11, 12]. Consumer dependence on certain information sources, their inclination to pay for sustainable goods, and their confidence in digital technology all influence market demand greatly [51, 61]. These elements taken together help to support environmentally friendly farming methods. A complex interaction of elements defines the path of agricultural sustainability: technology, legislation, farmer traits, and customer preferences among others.

Role of Mediators

In the complicated framework of agricultural sustainability, several intermediary variables are absolutely crucial in transforming the effect of individual elements into observable outcomes. Knowledge and skills become absolutely essential for the efficient application of creative agricultural practices as farmers' awareness of technology and related advantages, in addition to their competency in operating and supervising digital tools, transform into critical intermediaries [10, 12, 50]. Farmers' decision-making processes are complex and involve intermediaries such as risk perception, trade-off evaluation, trust, and adherence to social norms [12, 15, 36]. These several components work together to affect farmers' willingness to use new technology and sustainable practices, therefore acting as essential agents in the change towards agriculture more sensitive to the environment.

Furthermore, institutional support becomes clear as a necessary middle ground in this complicated equation. By bridging knowledge gaps, technical support, extension services, and training programs provided by academic institutions help to enable the adoption of sustainable agricultural methods [3, 9, 69]. By means of the required resources and assistance, institutions enable farmers to negotiate the complexity of technological adoption and sustainable farming, therefore contributing to the general success of sustainable agricultural projects [33, 38]. Within this complex and ever-evolving interplay, the support of institutions, the expertise of experts, and the decision-making processes serve as intermediates that funnel the effect of many variables into the framework of agricultural sustainability.

Role of Moderators

In the intricate fabric of agricultural sustainability, context-specific modifiers are very vital as they dynamically affect the interactions among many factors [7, 23]. Climate, geography, infrastructure, and cultural norms as context-specific variables that substantially influence the efficacy and suitability of specific agricultural technologies and practices [9, 48]. The complexity of these contextual elements highlights the need for tailored solutions as what works in one setting may not be automatically applicable in another [1, 6, 7]. The many characteristics of these contextual factors add an additional degree of complexity that calls for adaptable and sophisticated strategies to promote environmentally friendly agriculture practices.

Furthermore, the classification of farmers is a context-specific modifier that differentiates commercial farmers, smallholder farmers, organic farmers, and others based on their distinct risk profiles, resources, and requirements [5, 43]. These variations in farmers help to temper the impact of policies and technology by highlighting the necessity of interventions catered to the particular situation and challenges faced by different agricultural communities [10, 38]. According to some studies [11, 12], the design of the agricultural value chain is an additional factor that contributes to the complexity of the situation. This is because the interplay of power dynamics may have a considerable influence on the ways in which farmers get resources. One important context-dependent mediator that determines how much interventions impact livelihoods and overall sustainability is the way these dynamics are arranged within the supply chain [12, 14]. In order to develop strategies that are both efficient and adaptable to the ever-changing characteristics of agriculture, it is essential to identify and navigate these intricate contextual elements [8, 13].

RESEARCH GAPS AND FUTURE SCOPE

To have a better awareness of the factors influencing the acceptance of digital agriculture technology [6, 12] Research should look at how different sizes of agricultural businesses embrace technology such as sensors, drones, and farm management software depending on their usability, affordability, and usefulness [7, 9]. This information can be employed to influence legislation, extension services, and educational activities, thereby facilitating the widespread adoption of sustainable technologies and overcoming obstacles [10, 38]. Investigating the application of blockchain technology in agricultural supply networks and precision farming calls for more investigation [37, 50]. For governments, businesses, and consumers alike, an examination of blockchain's capabilities to improve openness, traceability, and trust might provide important new perspectives. A more environmentally conscious agriculture industry has the potential to be promoted through the widespread implementation of blockchain technology, which has the potential to cultivate trust, improve product safety, and encourage fair trading practices [11 - 13, 26]. Analyzing the results of these tests in different agricultural communities helps guide the design of more tailored and successful therapies. Understanding how peer networks disseminate knowledge about new technologies and influence adoption choices can help one to better plan outreach projects and extension services [10, 12]. Finding ideal information routes helps enable customized communication to meet the particular needs of farmers [5, 43]. Considering contextual variables, data analytics and artificial intelligence (AI) may be used to forecast technology adoption patterns [8, 15]. These models may be applied to support the development of AI-powered precision agricultural methods enhancing resource allocation, crop monitoring, and yield forecasting as well as to offer information for policy interventions. Examining market-driven solutions—such as the effect of eco-labelling on customer choices and the acceptance of technology—can help to synchronize technological growth with changing consumer preferences [4, 11]. This therefore improves the likelihood of customer acceptance and application. Important study subjects are investigating the possibilities of creating technology to increase climate change adaptation and analyzing the efficacy of agroecological techniques in lowering the consequences of extreme weather events [2, 3]. The adoption of technology has to be thoroughly evaluated in terms of social, environmental, and financial aspects [14]. This may be accomplished by applying approaches such as life cycle evaluation [7]. A more sustainable food system may also be developed by looking at the use of circular solutions that give waste minimization top priority, resource reusing top priority, and promotion of regenerative activities top priority. From the gaps that are highlighted by the existing literature, several questions (Table **2**) have been raised to be solved in future research.

Table 2. Shows the research questions raised under each theme.

Theme	Research Questions
Adoption and Diffusion of Technologies	1. How can we accelerate the adoption of sustainable agricultural technologies among smallholder farmers?
-	2. What factors influence the diffusion of innovative farming practices within local communities?
-	3. How do social networks and peer interactions impact technology adoption rates?
Blockchain Technology and Transparency	1. What are the potential benefits of integrating blockchain technology into supply chains for agricultural products?
-	2. How can blockchain enhance traceability, reduce fraud, and improve transparency in food production and distribution?
-	3. What challenges exist in implementing blockchain solutions in agriculture, and how can they be addressed?
Precision Farming and Sustainability	1. How does precision agriculture contribute to resource efficiency, reduced environmental impact, and increased productivity?
-	2. What role do data analytics and sensor technologies play in optimizing crop management practices?
-	3. How can precision farming practices be scaled up to benefit both large-scale and small-scale farmers?
Farmer Information Needs and Adoption	1. What information channels (*e.g.*, mobile apps, extension services) are most effective in meeting farmers' needs?
-	2. How can personalized and context-specific information improve technology adoption rates?
-	3. What barriers prevent farmers from accessing relevant information about new agricultural practices?
Community Supported Agriculture (CSA) and Platforms	1. How can CSA models be adapted to leverage digital platforms for better communication and coordination between farmers and consumers?
-	2. What impact does direct farmer-consumer interaction through digital platforms have on trust and satisfaction?
-	3. How can CSA programs ensure equitable distribution of benefits among participating farmers?
Participatory Action Research and Agroecosystem	1. How can participatory research involving farmers lead to more sustainable agroecosystem management?
Restoration	2. What role do local knowledge and indigenous practices play in ecosystem restoration efforts?
-	3. How can collaborative research projects engage farmers as active partners in designing and implementing restoration strategies?

(Table 2) cont.....

Theme	Research Questions
Innovation Networks and Sustainability	1. How do innovation networks (*e.g.*, agribusiness partnerships, and research institutions) foster sustainable practices in agriculture?
-	2. What mechanisms facilitate knowledge exchange and technology transfer within these networks?
-	3. How can innovation networks promote inclusive and equitable access to innovations across diverse farming communities?
Circular Economy in Agriculture	1. What circular economy principles can be applied to minimize waste and maximize resource utilization in agriculture?
-	2. How can regenerative practices (*e.g.*, cover cropping, and organic matter recycling) contribute to a circular agricultural system?
-	3. What policy frameworks and incentives are needed to encourage circular practices among farmers and agribusinesses?

CONCLUSION

Thanks to digital technology, an unparalleled effort has started with the constant quest for a strong and sustainable agriculture system. Important issues have been investigated throughout this discussion of research, offering an understanding of the possibilities as well as the challenges inherent in incorporating digital technology into the agricultural industry. Still, it is important to realize that this marks simply the first part of a continuous effort. In order to address emergent challenges, adapt strategies to changing circumstances, and ensure that digital agriculture significantly contributes to a sustainable and equitable future for all, it is essential to engage in ongoing research and innovation.

With regard to the development of solutions unique to every situation considering the variety of agricultural systems and socioeconomic conditions, extra research activities should be directed. By customizing technology and approaches to fit specific situations, their effectiveness and relevance rise, therefore fostering a digital agricultural environment that is more whole and powerful. Moreover, maintaining the main focus of research should be guaranteeing the development of inclusiveness and confidence. Promoting an ethically sound and socially responsible digital agriculture mostly depends on ensuring fair access to resources, addressing issues with data privacy, and strengthening underprivileged groups.

One such essential topic of future research is clearly facilitating teamwork. Improving the collaboration among a variety of stakeholders, including researchers, policymakers, farmers, and technology developers, and fostering partnerships among them, can accelerate the innovation process and strengthen mechanisms for the exchange of knowledge. Cooperation ensures the inclusion of several points of view when deciding the direction of digital agriculture in addition to helping the collaborative creation of solutions.

At last, ongoing research has to pay top priority to the evaluation of long-lasting consequences by means of thorough models assessing the social, technical, environmental, financial, and technological consequences of digital agriculture as it develops. It is of the utmost importance to have a comprehensive understanding of these effects in order to optimize tactics, mitigate the potential negative consequences, and improve the positive contributions that digital technology may make to agricultural systems that are both robust and sustainable. Fundamentally, the pursuance of a digital agriculture that is both environmentally sustainable and constantly evolving requires a steadfast commitment to continuous research, innovative practices, and a comprehensive methodology that integrates a variety of contexts and stakeholder perspectives.

REFERENCES

[1] Paul J, Criado AR. The art of writing literature review: What do we know and what do we need to know?. J Bus Res 2020; 29(4): 101717.

[2] El Fartassi I, Milne AE, El Alami R, *et al.* Evidence of collaborative opportunities to ensure long-term sustainability in African farming. J Clean Prod 2023; 392: 136170.
[http://dx.doi.org/10.1016/j.jclepro.2023.136170]

[3] Kumar S, Raut RD, Nayal K, Kraus S, Yadav VS, Narkhede BE. To identify industry 4.0 and circular economy adoption barriers in the agriculture supply chain by using ISM-ANP. J Clean Prod 2021; 293: 126023.
[http://dx.doi.org/10.1016/j.jclepro.2021.126023]

[4] Bouman BAM. A conceptual framework for the improvement of crop water productivity at different spatial scales. Agric Syst 2007; 93(1-3): 43-60.
[http://dx.doi.org/10.1016/j.agsy.2006.04.004]

[5] Giller KE, Witter E, Corbeels M, Tittonell P. Conservation agriculture and smallholder farming in Africa: The heretics' view. Field Crops Res 2009; 114(1): 23-34.
[http://dx.doi.org/10.1016/j.fcr.2009.06.017]

[6] Barnes AP, Soto I, Eory V, *et al.* Influencing incentives for precision agricultural technologies within European arable farming systems. Environ Sci Policy 2019; 93: 66-74.
[http://dx.doi.org/10.1016/j.envsci.2018.12.014]

[7] Mariyono J, Dewi HA, Daroini PB, Latifah E, Hakim AL, Luther GC. Farmer field schools for improving economic sustainability performance of Indonesian vegetable production. Int J Prod Perform Manag 2022; 71(4): 1188-211.
[http://dx.doi.org/10.1108/IJPPM-09-2019-0445]

[8] Ramankutty N, Mehrabi Z, Waha K, *et al.* Trends in global agricultural land use: implications for environmental health and food security. Annu Rev Plant Biol 2018; 69(1): 789-815.
[http://dx.doi.org/10.1146/annurev-arplant-042817-040256] [PMID: 29489395]

[9] Klerkx L, Aarts N, Leeuwis C. Adaptive management in agricultural innovation systems: The interactions between innovation networks and their environment. Agric Syst 2010; 103(6): 390-400.
[http://dx.doi.org/10.1016/j.agsy.2010.03.012]

[10] Loureiro ML, Lotade J. Do fair trade and eco-labels in coffee wake up the consumer conscience?. Ecol Econ 2005; 53(1): 129-38.

[http://dx.doi.org/10.1016/j.ecolecon.2004.11.002]

[11]   Schut M, Klerkx L, Rodenburg J, *et al.* RAAIS: Rapid appraisal of agricultural innovation systems (part i). a diagnostic tool for integrated analysis of complex problems and innovation capacity. Agric Syst 2015; 132: 1-11.
[http://dx.doi.org/10.1016/j.agsy.2014.08.009]

[12]   Hayashi T, Hidaka K, Teshima S. Carsharing and IT Enabled Services. SRII Global Conf 2014.

[13]   Mangla SK, Kazancoglu Y, Ekinci E, Liu M, Özbiltekin M, Sezer MD. Using system dynamics to analyze the societal impacts of blockchain technology in milk supply chainsrefer. Transp Res, Part E Logist Trans Rev 2021; 149: 102289.
[http://dx.doi.org/10.1016/j.tre.2021.102289]

[14]   Gebbers R, Adamchuk VI. Precision agriculture and food security. Science 2010; 327(5967): 828-31.
[http://dx.doi.org/10.1126/science.1183899] [PMID: 20150492]

[15]   Brunori G, Rossi A, Guidi F. On the new social relations around and beyond food. analysing consumers' role and action in gruppi di acquisto solidale (solidarity purchasing groups). Sociol Ruralis 2012; 52(1): 1-30.
[http://dx.doi.org/10.1111/j.1467-9523.2011.00552.x]

[16]   Carrer MJ, Filho HMS, Vinholis MMB, Mozambani CI. Precision agriculture adoption and technical efficiency: An analysis of sugarcane farms in Brazil. Technol Forecast Soc Change 2022; 177: 121510.
[http://dx.doi.org/10.1016/j.techfore.2022.121510]

[17]   Petticrew M, Roberts H. Systematic reviews in the social sciences. Malden: Blackwell Publishing 2006.
[http://dx.doi.org/10.1002/9780470754887]

[18]   Snyder H. Literature review as a research methodology: An overview and guidelines. J Bus Res 2019; 104: 333-9.
[http://dx.doi.org/10.1016/j.jbusres.2019.07.039]

[19]   Tranfield D, Denyer D, Smart P. Towards a methodology for developing evidence-informed management knowledge by means of systematic review. Br J Manage 2003; 14(3): 207-22.
[http://dx.doi.org/10.1111/1467-8551.00375]

[20]   Easterby-Smith M, Thorpe R, Jackson PR. Management Research. Sage 2012.

[21]   Anand A, Brøns Kringelum L, Øland Madsen C, Selivanovskikh L. Interorganizational learning: a bibliometric review and research agenda. Learn Organ 2021; 28(2): 111-36.
[http://dx.doi.org/10.1108/TLO-02-2020-0023]

[22]   Aguinis H, Ramani RS, Alabduljader N. What you see is what you get? enhancing methodological transparency in management research. Acad Management Ann 2018; 12(1): 83-110.
[http://dx.doi.org/10.5465/annals.2016.0011]

[23]   Mongeon P, Paul-Hus A. The journal coverage of Web of Science and Scopus: a comparative analysis. Scientometrics 2016; 106(1): 213-28.
[http://dx.doi.org/10.1007/s11192-015-1765-5]

[24]   Gupta S, Modgil S, Gunasekaran A. Big data in lean six sigma: a review and further research directions. Int J Prod Res 2020; 58(3): 947-69.
[http://dx.doi.org/10.1080/00207543.2019.1598599]

[25]   Thürer M, Tomašević I, Stevenson M, *et al.* A systematic review of China's belt and road initiative: implications for global supply chain management. Int J Prod Res 2020; 58(8): 2436-53.
[http://dx.doi.org/10.1080/00207543.2019.1605225]

[26]   Filgueiras IFLV, Melo FJCD. Sustainability 4.0 in services: a systematic review of the literature. Benchmarking (Bradf) 2023.

[27]   Chabowski BR, Samiee S, Hult GTM. A bibliometric analysis of the global branding literature and a research agenda. J Int Bus Stud 2013; 44(6): 622-34.
[http://dx.doi.org/10.1057/jibs.2013.20]

[28]   Centobelli P, Cerchione R, Chiaroni D, Del Vecchio P, Urbinati A. Designing business models in circular economy: A systematic literature review and research agenda. Bus Strategy Environ 2020; 29(4): 1734-49.
[http://dx.doi.org/10.1002/bse.2466]

[29]   Gioia DA, Corley KG, Hamilton AL. Seeking qualitative rigor in inductive research. Organ Res Methods 2013; 16(1): 15-31.
[http://dx.doi.org/10.1177/1094428112452151]

[30]   Gernsheimer O, Kanbach DK, Gast J. Coopetition research - A systematic literature review on recent accomplishments and trajectories. Ind Mark Manage 2021; 96: 113-34.
[http://dx.doi.org/10.1016/j.indmarman.2021.05.001]

[31]   Ojansivu I, Hermes J, Laari-Salmela S. Business relationships in the industrial network literature: Three approaches and their underlying assumptions. Ind Mark Manage 2020; 87: 181-95.
[http://dx.doi.org/10.1016/j.indmarman.2019.11.016]

[32]   Rezaee Vessal S, Partouche-Sebban J, Schiavone F, Raïes K. We link, you link: Social alliances and community engagement among vulnerable consumers in oncology. J Bus Res 2022; 143: 36-45.
[http://dx.doi.org/10.1016/j.jbusres.2022.01.059]

[33]   Cartwright S, Liu H, Raddats C. Strategic use of social media within business-to-business (B2B) marketing: A systematic literature review. Ind Mark Manage 2021; 97: 35-58.
[http://dx.doi.org/10.1016/j.indmarman.2021.06.005]

[34]   Reid DA, Plank RE. Business marketing comes of age: a comprehensive review of the literature. J Bus-Bus Mark 2000; 7(2-3): 9-186.
[http://dx.doi.org/10.1300/J033v07n02_02]

[35]   Larson DM. Exact welfare measurement for producers under uncertainty. Am J Agric Econ 1988; 70(3): 597-603.
[http://dx.doi.org/10.2307/1241498]

[36]   Bullock DS, Desquilbet M. The economics of non-GMO segregation and identity preservation. Food Policy 2002; 27(1): 81-99.
[http://dx.doi.org/10.1016/S0306-9192(02)00004-0]

[37]   Kumari R, Prasad MNV. Medicinal plant active compounds produced by UV-B exposure. Sustainable Agriculture Reviews 2013; pp. 225-54.
[http://dx.doi.org/10.1007/978-94-007-5961-9_8]

[38]   Ayele S. Biotechnology and biodiversity debates and policies in Africa. Int J Biotechnol 2008; 10(2/3): 207.
[http://dx.doi.org/10.1504/IJBT.2008.018353]

[39]   Zhao G, Liu S, Lopez C, *et al.* Blockchain technology in agri-food value chain management: A synthesis of applications, challenges and future research directions. Comput Ind 2019; 109: 83-99.
[http://dx.doi.org/10.1016/j.compind.2019.04.002]

[40]   Shekar M, Hyder Z, Subandoro A, Dayton Eberwein J, Pereira A, Akuoku JK. An Investment Framework for Nutrition in Uganda 2016.
[http://dx.doi.org/10.1596/28499]

[41]   Hamidoğlu A, Gül ÖM, Kadry SN. A game-theoretical approach for the adoption of government-supported blockchain application in the IoT-enabled agricultural supply chain. Internet of Things 2024; 26: 101163.
[http://dx.doi.org/10.1016/j.iot.2024.101163]

[42]   Sharma R, Samad TA, Chiappetta Jabbour CJ, de Queiroz MJ. Leveraging blockchain technology for circularity in agricultural supply chains: evidence from a fast-growing economy. J Enterp Inf Manag 2021.

[43]   Desai H, Kantarcioglu M, Kagal L. A hybrid blockchain architecture for privacy-enabled and accountable auctions. IEEE Int Conf Blockchain 2019.
        [http://dx.doi.org/10.1109/Blockchain.2019.00014]

[44]   Kamilaris A, Fonts A, Prenafeta-Boldú FX. The rise of blockchain technology in agriculture and food supply chains. Trends Food Sci Technol 2019; 91: 640-52.
        [http://dx.doi.org/10.1016/j.tifs.2019.07.034]

[45]   Monteiro Moretti D, Baum CM, Ehlers MH, Finger R, Bröring S. Exploring actors' perceptions of the precision agriculture innovation system – A Group Concept Mapping approach in Germany and Switzerland. Technol Forecast Soc Change 2023; 189: 122270.
        [http://dx.doi.org/10.1016/j.techfore.2022.122270]

[46]   Finger R, Swinton SM, El Benni N, Walter A. Precision farming at the nexus of agricultural production and the environment. Annu Rev Resour Econ 2019; 11(1): 313-35.
        [http://dx.doi.org/10.1146/annurev-resource-100518-093929]

[47]   Bottazzi P, Seck SM, Niang M, Moser S. Beyond motivations: A framework unraveling the systemic barriers to organic farming adoption in northern Senegal. J Rural Stud 2023; 104: 103158.
        [http://dx.doi.org/10.1016/j.jrurstud.2023.103158]

[48]   Wang J, Chen Z, Xiong Z, *et al.* Effects of biochar amendment on greenhouse gas emissions, net ecosystem carbon budget and properties of an acidic soil under intensive vegetable production. Soil Use Manage 2015; 31(3): 375-83.
        [http://dx.doi.org/10.1111/sum.12202]

[49]   Mellon-Bedi S, Descheemaeker K, Hundie-Kotu B, Frimpong S, Groot JCJ. Motivational factors influencing farming practices in northern Ghana. NJAS Wagening J Life Sci 2020; 92(1): 1-13.
        [http://dx.doi.org/10.1016/j.njas.2020.100326]

[50]   Brown B, Llewellyn R, Nuberg I. Why do information gaps persist in African smallholder agriculture? Perspectives from farmers lacking exposure to conservation agriculture. J Agric Educ Ext 2018; 24(2): 191-208.
        [http://dx.doi.org/10.1080/1389224X.2018.1429283]

[51]   Maertens M, Oyinbo O, Abdoulaye T, Chamberlin J. Sustainable maize intensification through site-specific nutrient management advice: Experimental evidence from Nigeria. Food Policy 2023; 121: 102546.
        [http://dx.doi.org/10.1016/j.foodpol.2023.102546] [PMID: 38130412]

[52]   Wang W, Mei T. Research on the effect of digital economy development on the carbon emission intensity of agriculture. Sustainability (Basel) 2024; 16(4): 1457.
        [http://dx.doi.org/10.3390/su16041457]

[53]   Kilelu CW, Klerkx L, Leeuwis C. Unravelling the role of innovation platforms in supporting co-evolution of innovation: Contributions and tensions in a smallholder dairy development programme. Agric Syst 2013; 118: 65-77.
        [http://dx.doi.org/10.1016/j.agsy.2013.03.003]

[54]   Mota J, Santos JN, Alencar R. Intertwining innovation and business networks for sustainable agricultural systems: A case study of carbon-neutral beef. Technol Forecast Soc Change 2023; 190: 122429.
        [http://dx.doi.org/10.1016/j.techfore.2023.122429]

[55]   Afzal A, Kilpatrick S, Turner LR. Tasmanian dairy farmers' attitudes towards using e-extension methods; strengthening the dairy extension system for a sustainable dairy industry in tasmania, australia. Sustainability (Basel) 2022; 14(21): 14585.

[http://dx.doi.org/10.3390/su142114585]

[56] Noga SR, Kolawole OD, Thakadu OT, Masunga GS. 'Wildlife officials only care about animals': Farmers' perceptions of a Ministry-based extension delivery system in mitigating human-wildlife conflicts in the Okavango Delta, Botswana. J Rural Stud 2018; 61: 216-26.
[http://dx.doi.org/10.1016/j.jrurstud.2018.06.003]

[57] Vanni F. Agriculture and Public Goods 2014.

[58] Altoaimy L. Driving change on twitter: a corpus-assisted discourse analysis of the twitter debates on the saudi ban on women driving. Soc Sci (Basel) 2018; 7(5): 81.
[http://dx.doi.org/10.3390/socsci7050081]

[59] Tandon S, Vishwanath T. The evolution of poor food access over the course of the conflict in Yemen. World Dev 2020; 130: 104922.
[http://dx.doi.org/10.1016/j.worlddev.2020.104922]

[60] Egelyng H. Managing agricultural biotechnology for sustainable development: the case of semi-arid India. Int J Biotechnol 2000; 2(4): 342.
[http://dx.doi.org/10.1504/IJBT.2000.000144]

[61] Bhargava AK, Lybbert TJ, Spielman D. Public benefits of private technology adoption: spatial externalities of water conservation in India. Water Econ Policy 2023; 9(02).

[62] Kinniburgh F. The politics of expertise in assessing alternatives to glyphosate in France. Environ Sci Policy 2023; 145: 60-72.
[http://dx.doi.org/10.1016/j.envsci.2023.01.017]

[63] Clark TN. The New. Polít Cult 2018.

[64] Gou F, Yin W, Hong Y, *et al.* On yield gaps and yield gains in intercropping: Opportunities for increasing grain production in northwest China. Agric Syst 2017; 151: 96-105.
[http://dx.doi.org/10.1016/j.agsy.2016.11.009]

[65] Venettacci S, Ponticelli GS, Guarino S. Fluidised bed finishing process for aeronautical applications: Environmental and technical-economic assessment. J Clean Prod 2021; 299: 126900.
[http://dx.doi.org/10.1016/j.jclepro.2021.126900]

[66] Berti G, Mulligan C. Competitiveness of small farms and innovative food supply chains: the role of food hubs in creating sustainable regional and local food systems. Sustainability (Basel) 2016; 8(7): 616.
[http://dx.doi.org/10.3390/su8070616]

[67] Bryant ST, Straker K, Wrigley C. The typologies of power: Energy utility business models in an increasingly renewable sector. J Clean Prod 2018; 195: 1032-46.
[http://dx.doi.org/10.1016/j.jclepro.2018.05.233]

[68] Silva THH, Sehnem S. Industry 4.0 and the circular economy: integration opportunities generated by startups. Logistics 2022; 6(1): 14.
[http://dx.doi.org/10.3390/logistics6010014]

[69] Hoof BV, Solano A, Riaño J, Mendez C, Medaglia AL. Decision-making for circular economy implementation in agri-food systems: A transdisciplinary case study of cacao in Colombia. J Clean Prod 2024; 434: 140307.
[http://dx.doi.org/10.1016/j.jclepro.2023.140307]

CHAPTER 5

Automating Agriculture: Robotics and AI for a Greener Future

Hemanth Kumar Shankarappa[1,*] and **Veluswamy Saravana Kumar**[1]

[1] *Acharya Institute of Management and Sciences, Bengaluru, India*

Abstract: This chapter delves into the transformative impact of robotics and artificial intelligence (AI) on modern agriculture, highlighting how these technologies are revolutionizing farming practices to achieve greater sustainability. Robotics in agriculture include the deployment of autonomous tractors, robotic harvesters, and precision weed control systems. These machines enhance efficiency, reduce labor costs, and minimize the use of harmful chemicals by targeting weeds and pests with unparalleled accuracy.

AI applications in agriculture extend to predictive analytics for crop management, smart irrigation systems, and real-time monitoring of crop health. Machine learning algorithms analyze vast datasets from sensors and satellite imagery to optimize planting schedules, irrigation, and fertilization, ensuring that resources are used judiciously and crop yields are maximized.

This chapter will explore real-world applications of robotics and AI in sustainable farming, examining their potential to address critical challenges such as climate change, soil degradation, and labor shortages. By integrating advanced technologies, farmers can achieve a balance between productivity and environmental stewardship, paving the way for a greener and more resilient agricultural future.

Keywords: Agriculture, Analytics, Artificial Intelligence (AI), Robotics, Sustainable farming.

INTRODUCTION

The rapid advancements in robotics and artificial intelligence (AI) are reshaping industries worldwide, and agriculture is no exception. Historically, farming has relied heavily on manual labor and traditional practices. However, with the increasing pressures of climate change, soil degradation, and population growth, agriculture has reached a turning point. To sustain future food demands,

---

* **Corresponding author Hemanth Kumar Shankarappa:** Acharya Institute of Management and Sciences, Bengaluru, India; E-mail: hemanthkumar.s@theaims.ac.in

Raghavendra M. Devadas, Vani Hiremani, Praveen Gujjar Jagannath, Lubna Ambreen & Harold Andrew Patrick (Eds.)

innovative approaches that increase productivity while maintaining environmental stewardship are essential. Robotics and AI represent key technological solutions that can address these pressing challenges, transforming agriculture into a more efficient, precise, and sustainable sector.

Globally, the agricultural industry is facing significant hurdles. According to the Food and Agriculture Organization (FAO) [1], by 2050, the world will need to produce 60% more food to feed a projected population of 9.7 billion people. Traditional farming methods, heavily reliant on intensive resource use, are proving insufficient. Furthermore, climate change is disrupting crop yields and exacerbating issues such as water scarcity and soil erosion. As a result, the adoption of innovative technologies such as robotics and AI is critical for enhancing productivity and resilience in agriculture.

Automation in agriculture is not a novel concept. Mechanization, in the form of tractors and other farming equipment, revolutionized farming during the 20th century. However, today's technological leap into robotics and AI-driven solutions is more profound, offering farmers the ability to optimize nearly every aspect of crop production with unprecedented precision. Autonomous machines are now capable of performing labor-intensive tasks such as planting, weeding, and harvesting, while AI applications are empowering farmers to make data-driven decisions, improving resource management and crop health monitoring. This chapter explores how these innovations are reshaping modern agriculture and paving the way for a more sustainable future.

The Role of Agriculture in the Global Economy

Agriculture remains a cornerstone of the global economy. According to the World Bank, the sector contributes approximately 4% of global GDP, with this figure rising to over 25% in some developing countries. As the world's population grows, the demand for food, fiber, and biofuels will continue to rise, putting further strain on agricultural systems. This makes the integration of cutting-edge technology not just an opportunity but a necessity for maintaining food security.

Robotics and AI are emerging as game-changers in agriculture, addressing critical issues such as labor shortages, rising input costs, and environmental degradation. The efficiency, precision, and adaptability offered by these technologies enable farmers to optimize their operations, reducing waste and increasing yields. Moreover, the environmental benefits of these technologies—such as reduced chemical usage, lower greenhouse gas emissions, and improved water efficiency—align with global sustainability goals, such as the United Nations Sustainable Development Goals (SDGs), particularly SDG [2], which aims to end hunger, achieve food security, and promote sustainable agriculture.

ROBOTICS IN AGRICULTURE

Autonomous Tractors and Machinery

One of the most significant breakthroughs in agricultural robotics is the development of autonomous tractors. These tractors operate with minimal human intervention, using GPS systems, sensors, and AI algorithms to navigate fields, plant seeds, and manage crops. John Deere, a pioneer in the field, introduced the first fully autonomous tractor capable of performing tillage with precision. Equipped with 360-degree cameras and advanced AI, these machines can continuously monitor their surroundings, making real-time decisions to avoid obstacles and optimize their routes.

The deployment of autonomous tractors can lead to significant cost savings for farmers. For example, labor costs, which represent a substantial portion of agricultural expenses, can be reduced by up to 60%. Additionally, the precision offered by these machines ensures that tasks such as planting and fertilizing are carried out with optimal accuracy, reducing the wastage of seeds and inputs. According to a report by Markets and Markets, the autonomous tractor market is expected to grow from USD 2.4 billion in 2021 to USD 6.5 billion by 2026, reflecting the growing demand for such technologies.

Robotic Harvesters

Robotic harvesters are another key innovation in agricultural automation. These machines are designed to identify and pick crops with remarkable accuracy, significantly reducing post-harvest losses. Traditional manual harvesting is not only labor-intensive but also prone to inefficiencies, leading to damaged produce. Robotic harvesters, equipped with machine vision and AI algorithms, can differentiate between ripe and unripe fruits or vegetables, ensuring that only the right crops are harvested at the right time.

For instance, Abundant Robotics, a U.S.-based company, has developed a robotic apple harvester that uses vacuum technology to gently pluck apples from trees without causing damage. This innovation addresses the problem of labor shortages in the fruit-picking industry while also improving the quality of the harvested produce. In Europe, robotic systems have been developed for harvesting delicate crops such as strawberries and tomatoes, which are particularly challenging to pick manually without damage.

Precision Weed Control

Weed management is one of the most resource-intensive tasks in farming, often requiring large amounts of herbicides. However, over-reliance on chemical herbicides has led to environmental issues, including soil degradation and the development of herbicide-resistant weeds. Precision weed control robots are designed to address these challenges by using advanced sensors and AI algorithms to identify and target individual weeds with minimal chemical use.

Blue River Technology's "See & Spray" system is an excellent example of this approach [3]. The system uses machine learning and computer vision to distinguish between crops and weeds, allowing farmers to apply herbicides only where necessary. This targeted approach reduces herbicide use by up to 90%, significantly lowering costs and environmental impact. Moreover, the reduced chemical load on the soil helps preserve soil health, which is critical for long-term agricultural sustainability.

AI IN AGRICULTURE

Predictive Analytics for Crop Management

Artificial intelligence plays a crucial role in transforming agricultural data into actionable insights. By analyzing vast datasets collected from sensors, drones, and satellite imagery, AI algorithms can predict weather patterns, pest outbreaks, and optimal planting times. This allows farmers to make informed decisions that maximize crop yields while minimizing resource use.

For example, IBM's Watson Decision Platform for Agriculture uses AI to provide farmers with predictive insights tailored to their specific fields. By integrating weather data, soil health indicators, and historical crop performance, the platform generates recommendations for planting, irrigation, and fertilization schedules. In 2020, the platform helped farmers in the U.S. increase their corn yields by an average of 10%, demonstrating the significant potential of AI to enhance agricultural productivity.

Smart Irrigation Systems

Water scarcity is one of the most pressing challenges facing agriculture today. According to the United Nations, agriculture accounts for approximately 70% of global freshwater withdrawals, making efficient water management critical for sustainability. AI-driven smart irrigation systems offer a solution by optimizing water usage based on real-time data from soil moisture sensors, weather forecasts, and crop needs.

Netafim, a leading provider of irrigation solutions, has developed AI-powered drip irrigation systems that deliver water directly to the roots of crops with pinpoint accuracy. These systems monitor soil moisture levels and adjust water flow in real-time, ensuring that crops receive the right amount of water at the right time. Studies have shown that smart irrigation systems can reduce water use by up to 30% while also improving crop yields by ensuring that plants receive consistent hydration throughout the growing season.

Real-Time Crop Health Monitoring

Monitoring crop health in real-time is essential for the early detection of diseases, nutrient deficiencies, and pest infestations. AI-powered systems, often integrated with drones and satellites, allow farmers to monitor large fields remotely and identify issues before they become widespread. This proactive approach reduces the need for chemical interventions and improves overall crop health.

For instance, SkySquirrel Technologies uses drone-based imaging systems to monitor vineyards. The drones capture high-resolution images of the crops, which are then analyzed by AI algorithms to detect signs of stress or disease. This allows farmers to take targeted actions, such as applying treatments only to affected areas, reducing the use of chemicals, and improving the quality of the final product.

THE IMPACT OF ROBOTICS AND AI ON SUSTAINABILITY

The global agricultural sector is under increasing pressure to balance productivity with sustainability. Traditional farming methods, particularly in industrialized agriculture, have contributed significantly to environmental issues such as deforestation, soil degradation, water pollution, and greenhouse gas emissions. Robotics and AI offer solutions that not only enhance productivity but also help mitigate these environmental impacts, creating more sustainable agricultural practices. This section delves deeper into how these technologies are contributing to sustainability.

Reducing Chemical Usage

One of the most significant environmental benefits of robotics and AI in agriculture is their potential to reduce the use of harmful chemicals, such as pesticides and herbicides. Conventional farming practices often involve broad-spectrum application of these chemicals across entire fields, resulting in overuse and runoff that contaminates soil and water bodies. Precision farming techniques, made possible by AI and robotics, allow for targeted application of chemicals only where they are needed.

The Blue River Technology "See & Spray" system, mentioned earlier, exemplifies this innovation. By using AI-driven machine vision, it identifies weeds at the individual plant level, allowing herbicides to be applied with pinpoint accuracy. This reduces chemical usage by up to 90%, not only lowering costs but also minimizing the environmental impact of chemical runoff. Such precision agriculture techniques are vital for protecting ecosystems and maintaining soil health in the long term.

Minimizing Water Waste

Water management is a critical challenge in agriculture, especially in regions prone to drought or water scarcity. Traditional irrigation methods often lead to over-watering or under-watering, both of which can negatively impact crop yields and contribute to resource depletion. AI-powered smart irrigation systems address this issue by using real-time data to optimize water usage.

Netafim's smart irrigation solutions, for example, ensure that crops receive the exact amount of water they need, reducing waste while maximizing crop health. According to research by the International Water Management Institute (IWMI), the adoption of AI-driven irrigation systems can reduce water usage by up to 30%. This is particularly important in water-stressed regions such as parts of India, Africa, and the Middle East, where efficient water management is critical to sustaining agriculture.

In addition to optimizing water usage, smart irrigation systems also help reduce the energy required to pump water, thereby decreasing greenhouse gas emissions. This dual benefit of water and energy efficiency makes AI-driven irrigation a key tool in promoting sustainable farming practices.

Improving Soil Health

Soil degradation is a growing concern in agriculture, with over-farming, erosion, and chemical overuse contributing to the loss of fertile land. According to the United Nations Convention to Combat Desertification (UNCCD), approximately 24 billion tons of fertile soil are lost each year due to erosion and poor land management practices. Robotics and AI can play a crucial role in improving soil health by promoting sustainable farming techniques.

For instance, AI-powered predictive analytics can recommend optimal planting and crop rotation schedules that prevent over-exploitation of soil. Robotic machinery, such as no-till seeders, can reduce soil disturbance, helping to maintain soil structure and prevent erosion. Additionally, AI systems can analyze soil data in real-time, identifying nutrient deficiencies or imbalances and enabling farmers to apply fertilizers more precisely, avoiding overuse and preventing nutrient runoff into nearby water bodies.

Reducing Carbon Footprint

Agriculture is responsible for approximately 25% of global greenhouse gas emissions, according to the Intergovernmental Panel on Climate Change (IPCC). Much of this is due to methane emissions from livestock, nitrous oxide from fertilizers, and carbon dioxide from agricultural machinery. By automating and optimizing farming practices, robotics, and AI have the potential to significantly reduce agriculture's carbon footprint.

For example, autonomous tractors and machinery powered by electric or hybrid engines can reduce the reliance on fossil fuels. AI systems that optimize fertilizer application can reduce the amount of nitrous oxide released into the atmosphere. Additionally, precision farming techniques can improve the efficiency of land use, allowing farmers to produce more food on less land and thereby reducing the need for deforestation.

In the long term, widespread adoption of these technologies could contribute to global efforts to combat climate change by making agriculture more carbon-efficient and less resource-intensive.

Enhancing Biodiversity

One often overlooked aspect of sustainable agriculture is the need to preserve biodiversity. Conventional farming practices, particularly monoculture, can lead to the depletion of biodiversity by encouraging the overuse of land for a single crop. This not only affects the local ecosystem but also makes crops more vulnerable to pests and diseases.

Robotics and AI can help promote more biodiverse farming practices. For instance, AI systems can analyze data on crop rotations and recommend planting patterns that encourage biodiversity. Robotic machinery can assist in managing diverse crops in a single field, a task that is labor-intensive and difficult to achieve manually. By fostering biodiversity, these technologies contribute to the overall health and resilience of agricultural ecosystems.

CHALLENGES AND BARRIERS TO ADOPTION

Despite the potential of robotics and AI to transform agriculture, several challenges remain in their widespread adoption. These challenges range from technical and financial barriers to ethical and social concerns. Understanding these barriers is crucial for developing strategies to overcome them and ensure that these technologies can be implemented on a global scale.

High Initial Costs

One of the most significant barriers to the adoption of robotics and AI in agriculture is the high upfront cost of these technologies. Autonomous tractors, robotic harvesters, and AI-powered systems require substantial investments, which may be prohibitive for small and medium-sized farmers, particularly in developing countries. For example, the cost of an autonomous tractor can range from USD 100,000 to USD 300,000, depending on the model and capabilities. Similarly, AI-powered analytics platforms often require ongoing subscription fees, which can add to the financial burden on farmers.

Governments and international organizations are beginning to recognize the need for financial support in this area. In some countries, subsidies and grants are available to help farmers adopt these technologies. However, more widespread financial assistance will be necessary to ensure that small-scale farmers, who make up the majority of the global agricultural workforce, can access these innovations.

Lack of Infrastructure

The successful implementation of robotics and AI in agriculture depends on a robust infrastructure that includes reliable internet access, data storage, and energy supply. In many rural areas, particularly in developing countries, these infrastructures are lacking. For example, AI systems often rely on cloud computing and real-time data analysis, which requires fast and reliable internet connections. In regions where internet access is limited or unreliable, farmers may be unable to fully utilize these technologies.

Additionally, the energy demands of autonomous machinery and smart irrigation systems can be a challenge in areas without a stable electricity supply. Renewable energy solutions, such as solar-powered equipment, may offer a partial solution, but these technologies also require upfront investment and maintenance.

Technical Integration

Even in regions with adequate infrastructure, integrating robotics and AI into existing farming practices can be challenging. Many farmers lack the technical expertise needed to operate and maintain these systems. Training programs and educational initiatives will be essential for helping farmers develop the skills they need to use robotics and AI effectively. This is especially true for older farmers who may be less familiar with digital technology.

Moreover, the integration of AI systems with existing farming equipment and software can be complex. Many farmers use legacy systems that may not be compatible with newer technologies. This creates a barrier to adoption, as farmers must invest not only in new machinery but also in upgrading their entire farm management system.

FUTURE PROSPECTS AND INNOVATIONS IN ROBOTICS AND AI FOR AGRICULTURE

As the adoption of robotics and AI in agriculture continues to grow, the future holds promising advancements that will further revolutionize the sector. These innovations aim to tackle challenges like food security, climate change, and resource efficiency while ensuring that agricultural practices remain economically viable and environmentally sustainable. This section explores some of the emerging trends and future prospects for robotics and AI in agriculture.

Next-Generation Autonomous Machinery

Autonomous machinery, while already making a significant impact, is expected to become even more advanced in the coming years. One area of development is the miniaturization of robots. Smaller, more nimble robots could be used to perform tasks that require delicate precision, such as tending to individual plants or working in environments where larger machines cannot operate. For example, companies like Small Robot Company in the UK are developing fleets of small, lightweight robots capable of planting, weeding, and monitoring crops without causing soil compaction, a significant problem with larger tractors.

Another exciting development is swarm robotics, where multiple small robots work collaboratively to complete agricultural tasks. These robots, often equipped with AI systems, can communicate with each other and adapt their behavior in real-time to optimize performance. Swarm robotics could revolutionize labor-intensive processes such as harvesting and weeding, making them more efficient and scalable.

The increased use of renewable energy in autonomous machinery is also on the horizon. As concerns about the environmental impact of fossil fuels grow, future robots are likely to be powered by renewable energy sources such as solar panels or biofuels. This shift will not only reduce the carbon footprint of agricultural operations but also lower operating costs for farmers, especially in remote areas where access to traditional energy sources is limited.

AI-Powered Drones and Aerial Systems

Drones, or unmanned aerial vehicles (UAVs), are already being used in agriculture for tasks such as crop monitoring, spraying, and data collection. However, future innovations will expand the capabilities of AI-powered drones, making them even more integral to precision farming. Advances in AI algorithms will enable drones to analyze real-time data more accurately, providing farmers with detailed insights into crop health, soil conditions, and pest activity.

One emerging trend is the use of multi-spectral and hyperspectral imaging in drones. These imaging technologies can detect changes in plant health that are invisible to the naked eye, such as water stress, nutrient deficiencies, or early signs of disease. AI systems can then process this data and provide farmers with actionable recommendations, allowing them to address issues before they become critical.

Additionally, the integration of drones with ground-based robotics is likely to become more common. For example, drones could work in tandem with autonomous tractors or robotic harvesters, providing real-time data to optimize their operations. This level of coordination between aerial and ground-based systems will enable even greater precision in tasks like spraying, planting, and harvesting.

AI-Driven Genetic Engineering and Crop Breeding

Artificial intelligence is also expected to play a transformative role in crop breeding and genetic engineering. As global populations grow and climate change intensifies, the need for resilient, high-yield crops is becoming more urgent. AI algorithms can analyze vast datasets of genetic information to identify traits that contribute to drought resistance, pest tolerance, and nutrient efficiency. This information can then be used to develop new crop varieties that are better suited to changing environmental conditions.

For example, AI is already being used by companies like Bayer and Syngenta to accelerate the breeding of new crop varieties. By analyzing data from field trials, climate models, and genetic research, AI systems can predict which combinations of traits will result in the most resilient and productive crops. This approach not only speeds up the breeding process but also ensures that new crops are optimized for specific environments and farming practices.

Furthermore, AI-driven genetic engineering has the potential to reduce the need for chemical inputs in agriculture. For instance, crops could be engineered to have natural resistance to pests, reducing the need for pesticides or fixing nitrogen from the atmosphere, reducing the need for synthetic fertilizers. These innovations will help make agriculture more sustainable and less reliant on external inputs.

AI-Powered Vertical Farming and Controlled Environment Agriculture

As the world's population continues to urbanize, there is increasing interest in vertical farming and Controlled Environment Agriculture (CEA), which allow crops to be grown in stacked layers or in fully enclosed environments such as greenhouses. AI is playing a crucial role in optimizing these systems by managing variables like light, temperature, humidity, and nutrient delivery with precision.

Vertical farming, which uses AI algorithms to control LED lighting systems, can mimic natural sunlight to optimize plant growth at different stages. This technology, combined with AI-driven irrigation and nutrient delivery systems, allows for year-round production with minimal water and land use. Moreover, vertical farming systems can be established in urban areas, reducing the need for long-distance transportation and contributing to food security in cities.

AI's role in CEA extends to automated crop monitoring. Sensors placed in these controlled environments collect vast amounts of data on plant health, growth rates, and environmental conditions. AI systems can then analyze this data and adjust the growing conditions in real-time, ensuring that crops receive the optimal conditions for growth. This level of control leads to higher yields, faster growth cycles, and reduced resource consumption, making CEA an important component of future sustainable agriculture.

POLICY SUPPORT AND GLOBAL INITIATIVES

While the technological advancements in robotics and AI for agriculture are promising, their successful implementation will depend heavily on supportive policies and global initiatives. Governments, international organizations, and private sector stakeholders all have a role to play in fostering an environment where these technologies can thrive. This section examines the key policy areas and global initiatives that are critical to driving the adoption of robotics and AI in agriculture.

Government Incentives and Subsidies

Governments around the world are beginning to recognize the potential of robotics and AI to address agricultural challenges. In many countries, including the U.S., Canada, and India, governments are offering incentives and subsidies to encourage farmers to adopt new technologies. These financial supports can take the form of tax credits, grants, or low-interest loans for purchasing autonomous machinery, installing AI-driven irrigation systems, or subscribing to agricultural analytics platforms.

For instance, the Indian government's "Digital Agriculture Mission 2021–2025" aims to leverage technology to improve agricultural productivity and sustainability. Under this initiative, farmers are provided with financial assistance to adopt AI-driven solutions and automation technologies. Similarly, in the European Union, the Common Agricultural Policy (CAP) offers financial incentives for farmers who adopt sustainable practices, including the use of precision agriculture technologies.

Moreover, governments are funding Research and Development (R&D) initiatives to advance the capabilities of robotics and AI in agriculture. Public-private partnerships are essential in this area, as they combine the resources of governments with the innovation of the private sector to develop cutting-edge technologies that can be deployed at scale.

Regulatory Frameworks for AI and Robotics

The rapid advancement of AI and robotics in agriculture necessitates the development of regulatory frameworks to ensure that these technologies are used responsibly. Issues such as data privacy, algorithm transparency, and the ethical use of AI need to be addressed by policymakers. For example, AI systems in agriculture often rely on vast amounts of data, much of which is collected from sensors, drones, and other monitoring devices. Ensuring that this data is used ethically and that farmers retain control over their data is critical.

In addition, regulations must be in place to ensure the safe operation of autonomous machinery. Countries like the U.S. and Germany have already begun to develop regulatory standards for autonomous vehicles in agriculture, focusing on issues such as safety, liability, and interoperability with existing farming systems. As more countries adopt these technologies, global standards and best practices will need to be established to ensure that robotics and AI are deployed in ways that maximize benefits while minimizing risks.

International Cooperation and Knowledge Sharing

The global nature of agricultural challenges, such as climate change, food security, and biodiversity loss, calls for international cooperation in the development and deployment of AI and robotics. International organizations like the Food and Agriculture Organization (FAO) and the World Bank are actively involved in promoting the use of technology in agriculture, particularly in developing countries where the need for innovation is greatest.

For instance, the FAO's e-Agriculture initiative aims to foster knowledge sharing and collaboration between countries on the use of digital technologies in agriculture. By facilitating the exchange of best practices and technical expertise, international cooperation can help ensure that AI and robotics are used to address global agricultural challenges in a way that benefits all regions.

Global initiatives such as the "AI for Good" platform, launched by the United Nations, also play a crucial role in promoting the use of AI to achieve the Sustainable Development Goals (SDGs). By aligning AI and robotics innovations with the SDGs, these initiatives ensure that technology is used to create a more sustainable, equitable, and resilient global food system.

CASE STUDIES: REAL-WORLD APPLICATIONS OF ROBOTICS AND AI IN SUSTAINABLE AGRICULTURE

To fully appreciate the transformative potential of robotics and AI in agriculture, it is essential to explore real-world examples where these technologies have been successfully implemented. This section highlights several case studies from different parts of the world that demonstrate the positive impact of robotics and AI on agricultural sustainability, productivity, and resource efficiency.

Case Study 1: Blue River Technology – Precision Weed Control

Blue River Technology, a U.S.-based company, has developed an innovative AI-powered solution for weed control known as "See & Spray." The system uses computer vision and machine learning to identify individual plants in real-time and precisely target weeds with herbicide, reducing the amount of chemicals needed by up to 90%. This not only minimizes the environmental impact of herbicides but also reduces costs for farmers.

The See & Spray system is mounted on tractors and uses cameras and sensors to scan fields at high speeds. The AI algorithm distinguishes between crops and weeds, ensuring that only the unwanted plants are sprayed. By targeting weeds with such precision, the system helps reduce chemical runoff into waterways, promoting more sustainable agricultural practices.

Blue River Technology's innovation has been particularly beneficial in large-scale farming operations where traditional weed control methods can be inefficient and costly. This case study demonstrates how AI-powered robotics can address environmental concerns while improving the economic viability of farming.

Case Study 2: Naïo Technologies – Autonomous Robots for Sustainable Farming

Naïo Technologies [4], a French company, has developed a range of autonomous robots designed to assist with various tasks in agriculture, from weeding and hoeing to harvesting. One of their flagship products, "Oz," is a small robot that can navigate fields autonomously, performing weeding tasks without the need for herbicides. This not only reduces the environmental impact but also decreases labor costs.

Oz is equipped with GPS and sensors to navigate accurately between rows of crops, ensuring that only weeds are removed while crops remain undisturbed. The robot is designed to work alongside farmers, who can program it to perform specific tasks based on the needs of their fields.

Naïo Technologies' robots have been deployed in vineyards, vegetable farms, and orchards across Europe, helping to promote organic farming practices and reduce the reliance on chemicals. This case study highlights the role of robotics in supporting sustainable, eco-friendly farming methods.

Case Study 3: John Deere – AI and Robotics for Autonomous Tractors

John Deere [5], a global leader in agricultural machinery, has been at the forefront of integrating AI and robotics into its products. One of their most significant innovations is the development of autonomous tractors equipped with AI-driven precision farming capabilities. These tractors can perform tasks such as plowing, planting, and harvesting without human intervention, using data from sensors and GPS systems to optimize their operations.

John Deere's autonomous tractors are designed to work 24/7, allowing farmers to maximize productivity and reduce the need for manual labor. The tractors are also equipped with AI systems that analyze data from the field, such as soil conditions and crop health, to adjust their operations in real time. For example, if the AI detects that certain areas of a field require more water or fertilizer, the tractor can apply these inputs with precision, minimizing waste and maximizing yields.

The success of John Deere's autonomous tractors demonstrates how AI and robotics can enhance the efficiency of large-scale farming operations while reducing resource consumption. This case study underscores the potential of automation to address labor shortages and improve the sustainability of agriculture.

Case Study 4: The Netherlands – AI and Robotics in Vertical Farming

The Netherlands is widely regarded as a pioneer in sustainable agriculture, and its use of AI and robotics in vertical farming is a prime example of how technology can transform food production. In urban areas, vertical farms are being developed where crops are grown in stacked layers inside climate-controlled environments. AI systems are used to manage lighting, temperature, and irrigation, optimizing conditions for plant growth.

One of the leading companies in this space, PlantLab [6], uses AI algorithms to analyze data from sensors that monitor plant health and growth rates. These AI systems can adjust environmental conditions in real time, ensuring that crops receive the optimal amount of light and nutrients. By growing crops in vertically stacked layers, PlantLab can produce up to 10 times more food per square meter than traditional farming methods, using 90% less water.

Vertical farming in the Netherlands has the potential to address food security challenges, particularly in densely populated urban areas where access to arable land is limited. This case study illustrates how AI and robotics can enable sustainable, high-yield food production in controlled environments, reducing the pressure on natural ecosystems.

CONCLUSION: A GREENER FUTURE THROUGH ROBOTICS AND AI IN AGRICULTURE

The integration of robotics and artificial intelligence into agriculture marks the beginning of a new era in farming—one that is more sustainable, efficient, and resilient in the face of global challenges. From autonomous tractors and drones to precision weed control and AI-driven genetic engineering, these technologies offer innovative solutions to some of the most pressing issues in modern agriculture, including labor shortages, climate change, and resource depletion.

As the case studies have shown, real-world applications of robotics and AI are already delivering tangible benefits in terms of increased productivity, reduced environmental impact, and improved resource efficiency. Whether through the precise targeting of inputs like water and fertilizer, the reduction of chemical use through automated weed control, or the optimization of growing conditions in vertical farms, these technologies are helping farmers achieve a balance between productivity and environmental stewardship.

However, realizing the full potential of robotics and AI in agriculture requires continued investment in research and development, supportive policy frameworks, and collaboration between governments, private sector stakeholders, and international organizations. Governments must provide the necessary incentives and regulatory frameworks to encourage the adoption of these technologies while also addressing concerns around data privacy, safety, and ethical AI use.

Furthermore, the success of robotics and AI in agriculture depends on knowledge sharing and capacity building, particularly in developing countries where the need for innovation is greatest. International initiatives that promote the transfer of technology and expertise will be crucial in ensuring that all regions can benefit from these advancements, helping to create a more equitable and sustainable global food system.

In conclusion, robotics and AI offer a pathway to a greener future in agriculture. By harnessing the power of these technologies, we can create farming systems that are not only more productive but also more resilient to the challenges of the 21st century. As the world grapples with issues like climate change, population growth, and food security, the role of robotics and AI in agriculture will only become more critical in shaping a sustainable and prosperous future for all.

REFERENCES

[1]   Food and Agriculture Organization (FAO). e-Agriculture and Sustainable Farming. 2021. Available from: https://www.fao.org

[2]   United Nations. AI for Good: Advancing Sustainable Development Goals. 2021. Available from: https://www.un.org

[3]   Blue River Technology. See & Spray: Precision Weed Control. 2021. Available from: https://www.bluerivertechnology.com

[4]   Technologies N. Oz: Autonomous Weeding Robot. 2021. Available from: https://www.naio-technologies.com

[5]   Deere J. Autonomous Tractors and Precision Agriculture. 2021. Available from: https://www.deere.com

[6]   PlantLab. Vertical Farming and AI. 2021. Available from: https://www.plantlab.com

CHAPTER 6

Advancements in Agricultural Technology

Veluswamy Saravana Kumar[1,*] and **Hemanth Kumar Shankarappa**[1]

[1] *Acharya Institute of Management and Sciences, Bengaluru, India*

Abstract: The agriculture industry has radically transformed over the past 50 years. Advances in machinery have expanded the scale, speed, and productivity. AI, analytics, connected sensors, and other emerging technologies could further increase yields, improve the efficiency of water and other inputs, and build sustainability and resilience across crop cultivation and animal husbandry. For the first time ever, food and agriculture took center stage at the annual United Nations climate conference in 2023 [1].

Emerging agriculture trends mark a shift towards smart farming and efficient utilization of time and resources while reducing crop losses. Smart farming is an upcoming trend that deploys technologies like the Internet of Things (IoT), computer vision, and artificial intelligence (AI) for farming. Robots and drones are accelerating farm automation by replacing manual farm operations such as picking fruits, killing weeds, or water spraying.

What are the new trends in agriculture?

As per 2023 status insights, impact of top 10 agritech trends & innovations in 2024 are Internet of Things (19%), Robotics (17%), Artificial Intelligence (14%), Agri Drones (13%), Precision Agriculture (11%), Agricultural Biotechnology (7%), Big Data & Analytics (6%), Controlled Environment Agriculture (6%), Regenerative Agriculture (4%) and Connectivity Technology (3%) [2].

Keywords: Agri drones, Connectivity technology, Innovations, Regenerative agriculture, Robotics.

INTRODUCTION

In addition to being the foundation of the majority of economies, agriculture is also essential to the world's sustainable future. This business has seen tremendous change over the last 50 years due to advancements in technology. Large-scale mechanical farming has replaced labor-intensive, manual methods, increasing agricultural yield, increasing efficiency, and drastically lowering manual labor.

* **Corresponding author Veluswamy Saravana Kumar:** Acharya Institute of Management and Sciences, Bengaluru, India; E-mail: saravanakumar.v@theaims.ac.in

Raghavendra M. Devadas, Vani Hiremani, Praveen Gujjar Jagannath, Lubna Ambreen & Harold Andrew Patrick (Eds.)

However, the agriculture industry faces a changing set of difficulties as populations continue to rise and pressure to provide food security increases. The need for sustainable farming methods, soil deterioration, resource shortages, and climate change are currently at the forefront of agricultural discourse.

Timeline Highlighting Major Agricultural Milestones

Up to 18th Century – Manual Agriculture: Tools and Manual Labour.

18th to 19th Century - Mechanization (Industrial Age): Tractors and Machines.

1960s to 1980s – Green Revolution (Chemical Fertilizers): Chemical Fertilizers and Hybrid Seeds.

21st Century – Digital Age (Smart Farming) Precision Farming, AI, Drones, *etc.*

These difficulties have prompted technology advancements that are starting to transform farming once more completely. In order to develop more effective, productive, and sustainable farming practices, new technologies and systems that utilize Artificial Intelligence (AI), Machine Learning (ML), robotics, the Internet of Things (IoT), and big data analytics are being incorporated into agricultural processes. These developments, which range from precision agriculture to controlled environment farming, are giving modern farmers with unprecedented opportunities to maximize their productivity while tackling the pressing problem of environmental sustainability.

This chapter will look at the several technical advancements that are now changing agriculture, emphasizing how they can help with the current issues facing the sector. Thanks to these advances, farmers can now reduce their environmental impact, improve resource efficiency, and enhance their resilience to the increasingly unpredictable effects of climate change.

SMART FARMING: THE FUTURE OF AGRICULTURE

As agriculture shifts toward data-driven decision-making, the idea of "smart farming" is gaining popularity. The use of technology, especially IoT, AI, and data analytics, to better and more sustainably manage agricultural processes is known as "smart farming." A science-based, analytical strategy that maximizes all facets of agricultural cultivation and livestock management is introduced by this method, which departs from old farming practices that mainly depend on guessing.

Internet of Things (IoT) in Agriculture

The Internet of Things (IoT) is transforming agriculture by enabling real-time monitoring and management of farming operations. Sensors, drones, and automated machinery are examples of Internet of Things devices that gather data on a variety of environmental parameters, including temperature, humidity, light levels, and soil moisture. After that, the data is sent to centralized systems for analysis and interpretation using AI algorithms. Farmers can use this information to make data-driven decisions on the exact state of their land and livestock.

IoT Application

a. Soil Sensors:

Function: Monitor moisture, nutrient levels, pH.

Benefits: Optimized irrigation and fertilization.

b. Weather Stations:

Function: Real-time weather monitoring.

Benefits: Adjust farming activities based on forecast.

c. Livestock Tracking:

Function: Monitor health and location of livestock.

Benefits: Improved animal welfare and management.

Source: https://iipseries.org/assets/docupload/rsl20244C713A6544F13E4.pdf

For example, smart irrigation is a popular use of IoT in agriculture. Sensors embedded in the soil monitor moisture levels and activate irrigation systems only when water is needed. This helps conserve water, which is crucial in areas with limited water supplies, by ensuring that crops are properly hydrated without being over-irrigated. A McKinsey & Company report claims that intelligent irrigation systems can save water use by as much as 30%, which promotes more environmentally friendly farming methods (McKinsey, 2022) [3].

IoT devices are being utilized in livestock farming to keep an eye on the behavior and health of the animals. Farmers might be warned of any health problems before they worsen by using wearable sensors that monitor vital signs, exercise levels, and dietary habits. This proactive approach to animal welfare not only improves productivity but also reduces the need for antibiotics and other interventions.

AI and Machine Learning in Agriculture

Artificial Intelligence (AI) and Machine Learning (ML) are critical to transforming agriculture into a precision-driven, highly optimised business. Farmers may make better decisions by using AI tools to interpret massive volumes of data from satellite photos, IoT devices, weather forecasts, and other sources. Predictive analytics, which uses historical data and machine learning algorithms to forecast crop yields, identify best planting times, and predict weather patterns, is an important application of AI in agriculture.

Farmers may reduce the risks associated with weather, pests, and illnesses by using predictive analytics. AI-powered systems, for instance, can examine weather trends and provide farmers with advance notice of impending storms or droughts so they can take precautions.

AI is also used in disease detection; computer vision systems equipped with machine learning algorithms can analyze images of crops and identify diseases or pest infestations at an early stage, allowing for timely intervention and reducing crop losses.

IBM's Watson Decision Platform for Agriculture is a noteworthy illustration of artificial intelligence in agriculture. It combines information from multiple sources, such as weather, soil sensors, and satellite photography, to give farmers useful insights. This platform ensures that resources are used effectively while reducing the impact on the environment by assisting farmers in optimizing their use of pesticides, fertilizers, and water (IBM, 2021) [4].

Crop breeding and genetic engineering are two more fields where AI is having a big influence. Genetic data can be analyzed using machine learning algorithms to find characteristics that increase crops' resistance to pests, diseases, and climate change. As a result, genetically engineered crops that are more resilient to harsh environmental conditions and use fewer resources have been developed, promoting more sustainable agricultural methods.

ROBOTICS AND AUTOMATION: REVOLUTIONIZING FARM OPERATIONS

Automation and robotics are being used more and more to do tasks that were formerly completed by hand as the agriculture sector struggles with manpower shortages and growing labor expenses. From planting and harvesting to crop spraying and animal monitoring, agricultural robots, or "agrobots," are transforming a number of farm tasks.

Robot Type

Harvesting Robots: Function: Automated harvesting of crops.

Weeding Robots: Function: Identifies and removes weeds.

Autonomous Tractors: Function: Autonomous planting and tilling.

Source:https://www.automate.org/robotics/blogs/robotics-in-agriculture-ty-es-and-applications

Agri Drones: Enhancing Aerial Surveillance and Precision Farming

In contemporary agriculture, agri-drones have emerged as one of the most popular developments. With the help of these drones' sophisticated imaging capabilities, farmers can monitor crop health, scan their fields from above, and spot symptoms of illness or stress. Drone-generated aerial imagery enables precise field mapping, allowing farmers to more easily identify areas that require additional water, fertilizers, or pest control.

Additionally, drones can be fitted with spray systems for precise application of insecticides, herbicides, and fertilizers. This focused strategy lowers operating expenses, minimizes environmental harm, and uses fewer chemicals. According to research in Agriculture and Human Values, using drones in agriculture can boost productivity while lowering labor and input costs by as much as 30% (Jones *et al.*, 2021) [5].

Drones are also employed in agriculture sowing. In order to ensure uniform dispersion and do away with the necessity for manual planting, specialized drones may shoot seed pods into the ground. This is especially helpful in reforestation initiatives or in locations that are hard to reach and where conventional planting techniques might not be feasible.

Robotics in Harvesting and Crop Management

The ability of agricultural robots to carry out intricate operations like pruning, weeding, and fruit and vegetable harvesting is growing. These robots use artificial intelligence and machine learning to identify ripe produce and harvest it with precision, minimizing damage to the plants. Robots can detect and delicately choose ripe strawberries, for instance, a duty that calls for both speed and dexterity. The labor-intensive task of weeding, which usually calls for the application of pesticides, is also being handled by robots. Reducing the need for chemical pesticides and encouraging more ecologically friendly farming methods, robotic weeders can detect and eradicate weeds using computer vision technology.

The ability of automation to lower labor costs in agriculture is among its most important advantages. Labor shortages are becoming a significant problem for farmers, especially in industrialized nations, according to a report by AgFunder Network Partners. Farmers can raise their total output, decrease their operational expenses, and lessen their dependency on manual labor by employing robots to carry out chores like weeding and harvesting (AgFunder, 2021) [6].

PRECISION AGRICULTURE: ENHANCING EFFICIENCY AND SUSTAINABILITY

Precision agriculture refers to the use of technology to monitor and optimize farming processes on a granular level. By leveraging data from sensors, drones, and satellites, precision agriculture allows farmers to apply water, fertilizers, and pesticides more precisely, ensuring that resources are used efficiently and sustainably.

Big Data and Analytics in Precision Agriculture

Precision agriculture relies heavily on big data and analytics. Farmers can learn more about crop health, soil conditions, and weather patterns by gathering and evaluating data from a variety of sources, including satellite imaging, weather stations, and soil sensors. With the help of these insights, comprehensive field maps that enable accurate input applications can be produced.

For example, farmers can use soil data to determine which parts of their fields need more water or nutrients, allowing them to apply water and fertilizer just where necessary. In addition to reducing waste, precision agriculture minimizes the environmental impact of farming practices. According to a PwC analysis (2022) [7], these systems can increase crop yields by up to 15% and reduce input costs by as much as 20%, making them a powerful tool for enhancing farm profitability.

Precision agriculture not only maximizes resource use but also assists farmers in reducing climate change concerns. Precision agriculture technologies can assist farmers in modifying their planting and harvesting schedules to take into consideration shifting weather patterns by evaluating past weather data and projecting future circumstances. This capability is especially important as climate change increases the frequency and severity of extreme weather events such as droughts, floods, and heat waves.

Controlled Environment Agriculture: The Rise of Indoor Farming

Growing crops indoors in a controlled environment, like a greenhouse or vertical farm, is known as Controlled Environment Agriculture (CEA). In order to provide ideal circumstances for plant growth, CEA systems employ cutting-edge technology to monitor and regulate environmental parameters like temperature, humidity, light, and CO_2 levels.

The ability to produce crops year-round, irrespective of weather conditions, is one of CEA's primary benefits. This is especially crucial in areas with severe weather or little arable land. CEA systems are a more sustainable choice for regions experiencing water constraints because they also consume a lot less water than conventional agricultural practices.

A kind of CEA called vertical farming is becoming more and more popular in cities where there is a high demand for fresh produce and limited space. Crops are grown in vertical farms using stacked layers, which enables high-density production in a compact space. These farms frequently use automated irrigation and nutrient delivery systems to guarantee ideal growing conditions, as well as LED lighting systems that simulate natural sunlight. By eliminating the need for long-distance transportation and lowering the carbon footprint of food supply chains, indoor farming has the potential to completely transform food production in urban settings.

AGRI-TECH STARTUPS AND THEIR ROLE IN INNOVATION

One of the driving forces behind technological innovation in agriculture is the emergence of agri-tech startups. These startups are leveraging cutting-edge technologies to solve pressing agricultural challenges and bring new tools to farmers worldwide. From precision farming to AI-powered decision-making systems, these companies are helping bridge the gap between traditional farming methods and modern technological advancements.

Startups such as Blue River Technology, which is now acquired by John Deere, are reinventing weed control. Their See & Spray technology employs computer vision and machine learning to distinguish between crops and weeds. This enables farmers to target weeds specifically with herbicides, lowering chemical use by up to 90%. Similarly, CropX, an Israeli agri-tech business, has created soil sensors that can measure moisture, salinity, and temperature in real-time. The acquired data is processed using AI algorithms to offer farmers actionable insights, helping them to make better irrigation and fertilization decisions.

In India, startups like **NinjaCart** and **Fasal** are pioneering new approaches to agricultural supply chain management and precision farming, respectively. NinjaCart connects farmers directly with retailers and wholesalers, eliminating intermediaries and ensuring farmers get better prices for their produce. Fasal, on the other hand, uses IoT sensors to monitor environmental conditions and provide farmers with real-time insights into their crops' health and growth patterns.

The rise of these startups is a testament to the importance of innovation in the agricultural sector. These companies are not only helping farmers optimize their operations but are also driving sustainability by reducing waste, improving resource efficiency, and minimizing the environmental impact of farming practices.

AGRICULTURAL BIOTECHNOLOGY: ENHANCING CROP RESILIENCE

Agricultural biotechnology is another significant area of technological innovation in agriculture. It involves the use of scientific tools and techniques, including genetic engineering, molecular markers, and tissue culture, to modify living organisms—primarily crops and livestock—so that they exhibit desirable traits such as improved resistance to pests, diseases, and environmental stresses.

Genetically Modified Crops (GMOs)

Genetically Modified Organisms (GMOs) are one of the most contentious but significant innovations in modern agriculture. Scientists can insert features into crops' genetic makeup that make them more resistant to herbicides, pests, and diseases, as well as improve their tolerance to harsh environmental circumstances like drought or salinity.

For example, BT cotton, a genetically engineered cotton type that generates an insecticidal protein derived from the Bacillus thuringiensis bacterium, is widely used in India and the United States. BT cotton is resistant to the bollworm, a significant pest that reduces cotton output. As a result, farmers that use BT cotton have reported higher yields and less reliance on chemical pesticides.

Similarly, Golden Rice, a genetically modified rice type containing beta-carotene, seeks to alleviate vitamin A deficiency, which is common in many impoverished nations. The introduction of GMOs such as Golden Rice demonstrates how biotechnology can help solve not only agricultural production but also larger health and nutrition issues.

Despite the potential benefits of GMOs, the technology has received criticism and mistrust from a variety of sources, particularly because of worries about food safety, environmental effects, and ethical reasons. As the debate over GMOs continues, it is obvious that agricultural biotechnology will play an increasingly important role in food production, especially as the world's population grows.

CRISPR Technology and the Future of Crop Breeding

In recent years, CRISPR-Cas9 has emerged as a groundbreaking gene-editing tool with the potential to transform crop breeding. Unlike traditional genetic modification methods, which typically involve adding foreign genes to an organism, CRISPR allows scientists to make precise changes to an organism's DNA—whether by removing, adding, or modifying specific genetic material. This precision enables the development of crops that are better equipped to handle environmental challenges and offer improved nutritional benefits, all without introducing foreign DNA.

For instance, CRISPR is being used to develop rice varieties with increased resistance to flooding—a growing concern as climate change makes extreme weather events more frequent. In addition, CRISPR is being leveraged to enhance the nutritional value of crops such as tomatoes and potatoes, which could play a key role in combating micronutrient deficiencies in populations that rely on these staple foods.

The potential applications of CRISPR in agriculture are vast, and the technology offers a promising solution to many of the challenges faced by modern farmers. However, regulatory frameworks around gene-editing technologies are still evolving, and it remains to be seen how quickly CRISPR will be adopted on a large scale.

REGENERATIVE AGRICULTURE: A HOLISTIC APPROACH TO FARMING

While much technological innovation in agriculture has concentrated on boosting productivity and efficiency, there is a rising shift towards regenerative agriculture, which prioritizes the restoration and enhancement of ecosystems through sustainable farming methods. This approach aims to improve soil health, promote biodiversity, and enhance water retention while also capturing carbon and helping to mitigate climate change. Regenerative agriculture focuses on farming practices that not only sustain but actively restore the environment, creating a more resilient and sustainable agricultural system for the future.

Soil Health and Carbon Sequestration

Improving soil health is a basic principle of regenerative agriculture. Healthy soils are vital for sustainable food production because they not only offer nutrients to crops but also regulate water cycles and trap carbon from the atmosphere. Cover cropping, crop rotation, no-till farming, and composting all improve soil structure, minimize erosion and increase organic matter content, resulting in higher crop yields and long-term sustainability.

Carbon sequestration, the process of capturing and storing atmospheric carbon dioxide, is another key focus of regenerative agriculture. By increasing the amount of organic matter in the soil, farmers can help draw down excess carbon from the atmosphere, thereby mitigating the effects of climate change. According to a study by the *Rodale Institute*, regenerative agricultural practices have the potential to sequester more than 100% of current annual CO_2 emissions if implemented on a global scale (Rodale Institute, 2020).

Biodiversity and Ecosystem Services

Regenerative agriculture also places a strong emphasis on biodiversity, both above and below the soil. A diverse ecosystem is more resilient to pests, diseases, and environmental stressors, making it better equipped to handle the challenges brought on by climate change. Practices like agroforestry—where trees and shrubs are integrated into crop and livestock systems—and Integrated Pest Management (IPM), which utilizes biological control methods to manage pests, contribute to increasing biodiversity on farms and improving ecosystem services.

Incorporating biodiversity into farming not only helps the environment but also boosts farm productivity and profitability. For example, agroforestry systems provide farmers with additional income streams from products like fruits, nuts, or timber while also enhancing soil fertility and water retention. This holistic approach not only sustains the land but also supports farmers' long-term financial success.

The Role of Technology in Supporting Regenerative Agriculture

While regenerative agriculture relies on traditional, nature-based solutions, technology can help scale these techniques. Satellite imaging and remote sensing technology, for example, can be used to track soil health, carbon sequestration, and the long-term effectiveness of regeneration techniques. Furthermore, big data analytics can assist farmers in determining the most successful regenerative techniques for their individual conditions and tracking advances in soil health and biodiversity. The combination of regenerative agriculture and technology is a comprehensive strategy for farming that not only increases productivity but also strengthens agricultural systems' resilience to climate change and other problems.

CONNECTIVITY TECHNOLOGY: BRIDGING THE DIGITAL DIVIDE

For technological innovations in agriculture to be effective, it is essential that farmers, particularly in rural areas, have access to reliable **connectivity technology**. Unfortunately, many farmers around the world still lack access to the internet or digital infrastructure, limiting their ability to adopt new technologies and access valuable data.

The Importance of Digital Infrastructure in Agriculture

Connectivity technology, such as broadband internet, cellular networks, and satellite communication, plays a vital role in enabling farmers to fully leverage IoT devices, data analytics, and AI-driven platforms. Without reliable internet access, farmers are unable to effectively monitor their crops and livestock, access real-time weather data, or use online platforms for selling their produce.

Governments and private companies are increasingly acknowledging the importance of enhancing digital infrastructure in rural areas. For example, Microsoft's Airband Initiative seeks to bring broadband internet to underserved rural communities globally. Similarly, Google's Project Loon has used high-altitude balloons to provide internet access to remote regions, including agricultural zones that lack conventional infrastructure.

Improving connectivity in rural areas is not just about providing internet access—it's about equipping farmers with the tools and information necessary to succeed in an increasingly competitive and technology-driven agricultural landscape.

BIG DATA AND ANALYTICS IN AGRICULTURE

The agricultural industry generates a tremendous amount of data, from soil moisture levels and weather patterns to crop health and yield estimates. The ability to harness this data through **big data analytics** is transforming the way farmers manage their fields and make critical decisions. Big data analytics refers to the use of advanced algorithms and statistical models to process and analyze large, complex datasets to uncover patterns, trends, and insights that can be used to optimize farming practices.

Data-Driven Decision Making

One of the key advantages of big data in agriculture is its ability to empower data-driven decision-making. By utilizing real-time data from IoT sensors, satellite imagery, and weather forecasts, farmers can make informed choices about planting schedules, irrigation, fertilization, and pest management. Additionally, by analyzing both historical and real-time data, farmers can predict future crop yields and market prices, enabling them to make more strategic financial and operational decisions.

For instance, John Deere has incorporated big data analytics into its precision agriculture platform, allowing farmers to collect and analyze data from their equipment and fields. This information helps optimize machinery settings, reduce fuel consumption, and improve crop yields. Similarly, The Climate Corporation offers a digital farming platform that uses big data and AI to deliver personalized recommendations tailored to the specific conditions of each field, enhancing farmers' ability to maximize productivity and sustainability.

Predictive Analytics for Crop Management

Predictive analytics, a subset of big data analytics, forecasts future outcomes by combining historical data with machine learning algorithms. In agriculture, predictive analytics can be used to forecast crop yields, pest and disease outbreaks, and changes in weather patterns. This enables farmers to take preventive measures to protect their crops while increasing yield.

For example, Corteva Agriscience uses predictive analytics to assist farmers in optimizing planting dates and selecting the optimum crop varieties for their fields. Corteva's technology uses data on soil conditions, weather patterns, and historical yields to anticipate which crops will perform best under certain conditions.

Application

Crop Yield Prediction

Forecasting future yields based on historical data and real-time inputs. It helps farmers plan ahead and allocate resources effectively.

Pest and Disease Prediction

Identifying the likelihood of pest or disease outbreaks based on environmental data. Allows for timely interventions, reducing crop loss.

Weather Forecasting

Predicting weather patterns and climate changes. Helps farmers adjust irrigation, planting, and harvesting schedules.

Improving Supply Chain Management with Big Data

Beyond the farm, big data is also being used to improve the efficiency and transparency of agricultural supply chains. By tracking the movement of goods from farm to market, big data analytics can help reduce waste, improve logistics, and ensure that products reach consumers as quickly and efficiently as possible.

In India, for instance, startups like **NinjaCart** use big data analytics to streamline the supply chain for fresh produce. NinjaCart's platform connects farmers directly with retailers, eliminating intermediaries and reducing food waste. The platform uses real-time data to predict demand, optimize delivery routes, and ensure that produce reaches retailers at the right time.

PRECISION AGRICULTURE: MAXIMIZING EFFICIENCY

Precision agriculture is a farming management concept based on observing, measuring, and responding to inter- and intra-field variability in crops. It involves using technology such as GPS, drones, and IoT sensors to gather data about soil conditions, crop health, and weather patterns to optimize agricultural practices.

Yield Mapping and Variable Rate Technology (VRT)

One of the key components of precision agriculture is **yield mapping**, which involves using GPS-enabled combine harvesters to map crop yields across different areas of a field. This data can then be used to identify patterns in crop performance and make more informed decisions about how to manage the field in the future.

Input

Fertilizer: **Benefits:** Reduced usage, cost savings.

Seeds: **Benefits:** Increased yields, optimized planting.

Another essential technology in precision agriculture is Variable Rate Technology (VRT), which enables farmers to apply inputs like fertilizers, pesticides, and water at different rates across a field, depending on the specific needs of each area. By customizing the application of these inputs to the unique conditions of various sections of the field, farmers can minimize waste, reduce costs, and enhance crop yields. This targeted approach not only optimizes resource use but also helps promote sustainability by reducing over-application and minimizing environmental impact.

Precision Agriculture Workflow

Data Collection

Drones, GPS, and IoT Sensors gather data on soil health, crop growth, and environmental conditions.

Data Analysis

Data is processed and analyzed using software and big data analytics.

Decision Making

Farmers receive actionable insights and recommendations.

Action

Variable rate technology adjusts inputs based on data-driven insights [8].

Drones in Agriculture

Drones are becoming increasingly popular in precision agriculture because of their capacity to capture high-resolution photographs of fields and track crop health in real-time. Drones outfitted with multispectral sensors may record precise photos that indicate changes in crop health, helping farmers detect nutritional deficits, water stress, and pest infestations early.

Drones can also be used to spray crops with pesticides or fertilizers, plant seeds, and even monitor livestock. For example, DJI, a leading drone company, sells agricultural drones such as the AGRAS MG-1, which can spray crops with fertilizer and insecticides autonomously, considerably lowering the time and effort required for these chores.

Application

Crop Monitoring

Capturing high-resolution images of fields. Early detection of crop health issues.

Precision Spraying

Autonomous spraying of crops with fertilizers/pesticides. Reduces labor costs and improves efficiency.

Livestock Monitoring

Monitoring livestock health and location. Saves time and improves herd management.

Smart Irrigation Systems

One of the most critical challenges in agriculture is the efficient use of water. **Smart irrigation systems** use IoT sensors, weather data, and predictive analytics to optimize water usage, ensuring that crops receive the right amount of water at the right time. These systems help reduce water waste, lower costs, and improve crop health.

For example, **Netafim**, a leader in drip irrigation technology, has developed smart irrigation systems that use soil moisture sensors and weather data to automatically adjust irrigation schedules based on the specific needs of each plant. This ensures that water is used as efficiently as possible, reducing water consumption and preventing over-irrigation.

THE ROLE OF GOVERNMENT AND POLICY IN AGRICULTURAL INNOVATION

While technological advancements in agriculture are largely driven by the private sector, governments and policymakers also play a critical role in supporting innovation and ensuring that farmers have access to the tools and resources they need to adopt new technologies. Governments can influence the adoption of agricultural technologies through subsidies, regulations, and infrastructure development.

Subsidies and Financial Incentives

One of the biggest barriers to adopting new agricultural technologies is the high upfront cost, particularly for small-scale farmers. Governments can help mitigate this by offering subsidies and financial incentives to encourage the adoption of technologies such as precision farming tools, smart irrigation systems, and drones.

For example, the Indian government offers various subsidies for the purchase of farm machinery and equipment through schemes such as the Sub-Mission on

Agricultural Mechanization (SMAM). These subsidies help reduce the financial burden on farmers and make it easier for them to invest in modern technology.

Infrastructure Development

Access to infrastructure, particularly digital infrastructure, is essential for the widespread adoption of agricultural technologies. Governments must invest in the development of rural broadband networks, cellular coverage, and power infrastructure to ensure that farmers in remote areas can take advantage of IoT devices, data analytics, and AI platforms.

For instance, countries like **Australia** and **the Netherlands** have invested heavily in digital infrastructure to support their agricultural sectors. By providing farmers with reliable internet access and modern infrastructure, these countries have positioned themselves as leaders in smart farming and precision agriculture.

Regulatory Frameworks

The regulatory environment also plays a crucial role in shaping the adoption of new technologies in agriculture. Governments must develop clear and consistent regulatory frameworks for technologies such as GMOs, CRISPR gene editing, and drones. These regulations should balance the need to protect consumers and the environment while allowing for innovation and technological progress.

For example, in the **European Union**, the regulatory environment around GMOs is highly restrictive, which has limited the adoption of genetically modified crops in many EU countries. In contrast, countries like the **United States** and **Brazil** have more permissive regulatory frameworks, which has led to higher rates of GMO adoption.

CHALLENGES AND FUTURE OUTLOOK

While the adoption of technological innovations in agriculture has the potential to transform the industry, there are several challenges that must be addressed. One of the primary challenges is the cost of implementing these technologies, particularly for small-scale farmers in developing countries. The high upfront costs of purchasing IoT devices, drones, and robotics can be prohibitive for farmers with limited financial resources.

Another challenge is the lack of technical expertise required to operate and maintain these technologies. Many farmers, particularly in rural areas, may not have the necessary training or access to technical support to fully utilize these innovations. This highlights the need for educational programs and government initiatives to support the adoption of agricultural technologies.

Despite these challenges, the future of agriculture is undeniably linked to technological innovation. As the global population continues to grow, the demand for food will only increase, and the agricultural sector must find ways to produce more with fewer resources. Technological innovations, such as AI, IoT, robotics, and precision agriculture, offer promising solutions to these challenges. By embracing these advancements, farmers can increase their productivity, reduce their environmental impact, and build a more sustainable future for agriculture.

CONCLUSION

Technological innovation in agriculture has the potential to revolutionize the way we produce food. From AI-powered predictive analytics and IoT-enabled smart farming to robotic harvesters and precision agriculture, these advancements are creating new opportunities for farmers to optimize their operations and address the challenges of climate change, resource scarcity, and environmental sustainability.

The future of agriculture will be shaped by the continued development and adoption of these technologies. By investing in innovation and fostering collaboration between farmers, researchers, and technology providers, we can build a more resilient and sustainable agricultural system that benefits both farmers and consumers.

REFERENCES

[1]   The role of food and agriculture in tackling climate change. United Nations Climate Conference Report 2023.

[2]   Agriculture: IoT & big data trends. Statista 2023.

[3]   Smart irrigation systems: reducing water usage in agriculture. McKinsey & Company 2022.

[4]   Watson Decision Platform for Agriculture: transforming farming with AI. IBM 2021.

[5]   Jones M. Agri drones: enhancing precision farming. Agric Human Values 2021; 38(3): 245-67.

[6]   The role of robotics in addressing labor shortages in agriculture. AgFunder Network Partners 2021.

[7]   The future of precision agriculture: big data and analytics in farming. PwC 2022.

[8]   Precision agriculture: increasing efficiency and sustainability. FAO Report 2021.

SUBJECT INDEX

Raghavendra M. Devadas, Vani Hiremani, Praveen Gujjar Jagannath, Lubna Ambreen & Harold Andrew Patrick (Eds.)

www.ingramcontent.com/pod-product-compliance
Lightning Source LLC
Chambersburg PA
CBHW041716210326
41598CB00007B/676